English for Listening, Speaking, Reading & Writing

NEW CONNECTION

BRING YOUR ENGLISH TO THE NEXT LEVEL

STUDENT BOOK 2

INTRODUCTION

Welcome to ***NEW CONNECTION*** — *BRING YOUR ENGLISH TO THE NEXT LEVEL.* This is the second book in a series created to propel learners toward fluency. Outstanding English skills will open up doors for anyone in today's world. No matter how out of reach a student's learning goals seem to be, the ***NEW CONNECTION*** series will provide the boost he or she needs.

Each unit of ***NEW CONNECTION*** — *BRING YOUR ENGLISH TO THE NEXT LEVEL* follows a set structure designed to push students to put what they have learned into practice as well as to challenge them to expand their skills. The unit begins with a **Words & Expressions** section, which utilizes both audio and visual methods to introduce words and expressions related to the topic. This is followed by a **Listen Up** exercise. At this time, learners will review vocabulary by answering questions based on a dialogue or monologue. The **Act It Out** section then gives learners a chance to put the vocabulary to use with a partner.

Students will move on to a video clip in which actors use new vocabulary — in addition to new grammar points and expressions — in real-life situations. They will listen along and fill in blanks too, and later be tested for comprehension. Afterwards, they're prompted to put freshly learned vocabulary and grammar skills to use in a series of review exercises. The unit ends with a related article and an opportunity for students to write their own compositions.

As students progress through each level, they are constantly encouraged to put what they have learned to use. At the same time, they never stop taking on new challenges to help themselves reach the next benchmark in the learning process. By developing a hunger for advancement, ***NEW CONNECTION*** — *BRING YOUR ENGLISH TO THE NEXT LEVEL* proves that the sky is the limit for today's learners.

CONTENTS

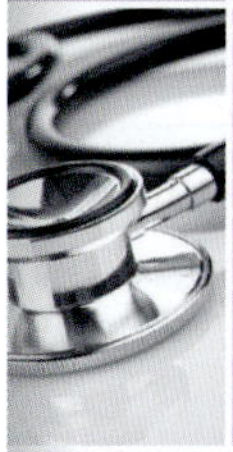

CONTENT CHART

Unit	Title	Subject	Conversation	Grammar
1	**Meeting People**	School Clubs	Good to Meet You / Meet the Coach	Simple Present Tense
2	**Time to Eat**	Food	Enjoy Free Food	Count Nouns vs. Non-Count Nouns
3	**Living with Technology**	Electronics	Homework or Video Games?	Present Continuous Tense
4	**Looking Good**	Physical Appearance	A Trip Home	Simple Past Tense
5	**Not Feeling So Good**	Symptoms	Feeling Sick?	Linking Verbs Causative Verbs
6	**The Big Screen**	Types of Movies	Movie Night	Talking about Time
7	**How Do You Feel?**	Feelings	Bad News, Good News	Participial Adjectives
8	**All in Good Fun**	Hobbies	Making Plans	Gerunds and Infinitives
9	**Game Time**	Sports	Sports Talk	Past Continuous Tense
10	**Rain or Shine**	Weather	A Weekend at the Lake	Simple Future Tense
11	**Eating Out**	Food	Dinner Date	Indefinite Pronouns
12	**School Life**	Characteristics	Tell Me What to Do	Conditionals

	Reading	Writing
Statements Third Person Singular Yes / No Questions Wh- Questions	A Strange College Club	Personal Profiles
Differences Plural Count Nouns Articles, Determiners & Quantifiers	Eat More and Lose Weight	Festivals
Statements Questions Verb + -ing Usage	It's a YouTube World	Internet Language
Be Verbs Verbs	Dangerous Beauty	Wanted Ads
Definition Usage	Natural Medicine for Your Cold	Medical History
Prepositions Questions Telling Time	The Wildest Job in Movies	Movie Reviews
Usage Paired Adjectives Past Participial Adjectives with Prepositions	Do Animals Have Feelings?	Life Stories
Usage Signal Words Different Meanings	Make Your Life More Extreme	Pastimes
Statements Questions Usage	Sports Hero	Favorite Sports
Statements Questions Be Going to vs. Will Future Time Expressions	Safe at Home	Storm Warnings
	Going to Restaurants around the World	Restaurant Reviews
Zero Conditional First Conditional Different Forms	Working for No Money	Job Applications

LEARNING OVERVIEW

UNIT 1 Meeting People

1. How did you meet your best friend?
2. What are some good places to meet new people?
3. Are you comfortable talking with people in English?

| Words & Expressions

Listen and write the sentence number of the activity in the box.

School Clubs

basketball, mountain climbing, chess, guitar, in-line skating, break-dancing, yoga, drama, swimming, movie, tennis, martial arts

Practice

Practice these sentence patterns using the words above.

- I'm in the ______ club.
- I want to join the ______ club.
- I'm a member of the ______ club.
- I participate in the ______ club.

| Listen Up

Task I *Listen and decide which club is the best for each person.*

Marie, Doug, Sharon, Adam

Task II *Listen again and choose the answers.*

1. Marie wants to become a break-dancer / hip-hop singer.
2. Doug watches / plays his favorite sport every day.
3. Sharon likes to stay indoors / be in nature.
4. Adam needs to practice in-line skating / skiing.

| Act It Out

Practice the conversations with the word choices given.

tennis	guitar	movie	drama
play tennis	play the guitar	watch movies	see plays

1. A: Are you in any school clubs?
   B: Yes, I am. I am in the ______ club.
2. A: I belong to the ______ club.
   B: Cool! I like to ______ too.
3. A: My favorite hobby is to ______.
   B: Then why don't you join the ______ club?

| Did You Know...?

Place the words from **Words & Expressions** *in the correct columns.*

do	play	go	others
			break-dance act watch movies

Listen Up

checks students' understanding of the words they have learned through listening comprehension questions.

Act It Out

helps students understand the key expressions and words by practicing short dialogues.

Did You Know...?

helps students expand their vocabulary through words and expressions.

Words & Expressions

provides useful items with audio support to further students' understanding of the topic.

Conversation

includes a video clip helping students understand the content.

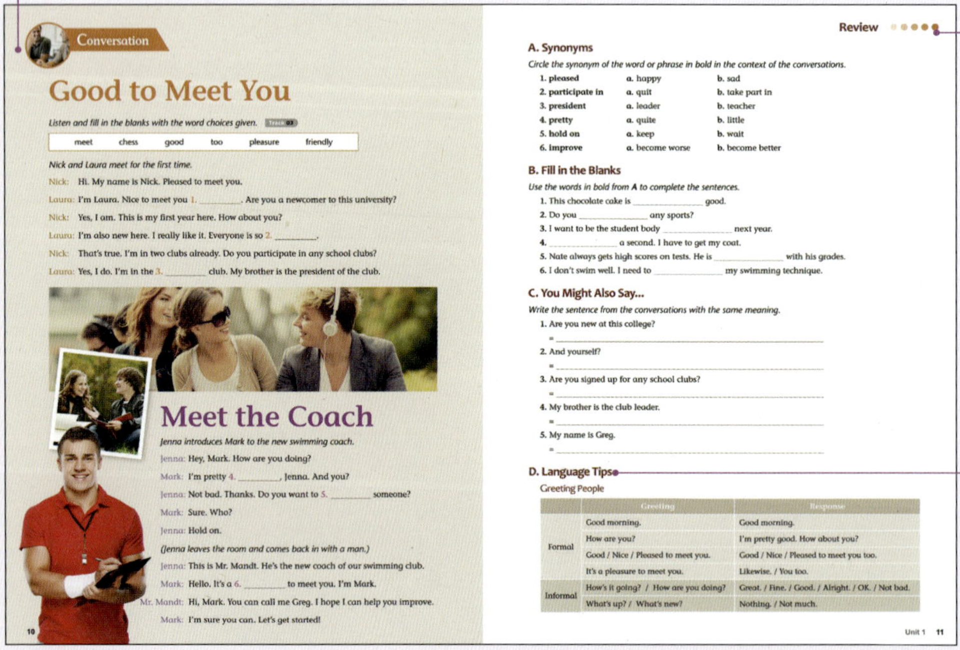

Conversation

Good to Meet You

Listen and fill in the blanks with the word choices given.

meet	chess	good	too	pleasure	friendly

Nick and Laura meet for the first time.

Nick: Hi. My name is Nick. Pleased to meet you.
Laura: I'm Laura. Nice to meet you 1. ______. Are you a newcomer to this university?
Nick: Yes, I am. This is my first year here. How about you?
Laura: I'm also new here. I really like it. Everyone is so 2. ______.
Nick: That's true. I'm in two clubs already. Do you participate in any school clubs?
Laura: Yes, I do. I'm in the 3. ______ club. My brother is the president of the club.

Meet the Coach

Jenna introduces Mark to the new swimming coach.

Jenna: Hey, Mark. How are you doing?
Mark: I'm pretty 4. ______, Jenna. And you?
Jenna: Not bad. Thanks. Do you want to 5. ______ someone?
Mark: Sure. Who?
Jenna: Hold on.
(Jenna leaves the room and comes back in with a man.)
Jenna: This is Mr. Mandt. He's the new coach of our swimming club.
Mark: Hello. It's a 6. ______ to meet you. I'm Mark.
Mr. Mandt: Hi, Mark. You can call me Greg. I hope I can help you improve.
Mark: I'm sure you can. Let's get started!

Review

A. Synonyms

Circle the synonym of the word or phrase in bold in the context of the conversations.

1. **pleased**	a. happy	b. sad
2. **participate in**	a. quit	b. take part in
3. **president**	a. leader	b. teacher
4. **pretty**	a. quite	b. little
5. **hold on**	a. keep	b. wait
6. **improve**	a. become worse	b. become better

B. Fill in the Blanks

Use the words in bold from A to complete the sentences.

1. This chocolate cake is ______ good.
2. Do you ______ any sports?
3. I want to be the student body ______ next year.
4. ______ a second. I have to get my coat.
5. Nate always gets high scores on tests. He is ______ with his grades.
6. I don't swim well. I need to ______ my swimming technique.

C. You Might Also Say...

Write the sentence from the conversations with the same meaning.

1. Are you new at this college?
   = ______
2. And yourself?
   = ______
3. Are you signed up for any school clubs?
   = ______
4. My brother is the club leader.
   = ______
5. My name is Greg.
   = ______

D. Language Tips

Greeting People

	Greeting	Response
Formal	Good morning.	Good morning.
	How are you?	I'm pretty good. How about you?
	Good / Nice / Pleased to meet you.	Good / Nice / Pleased to meet you too.
	It's a pleasure to meet you.	Likewise. / You too.
Informal	How's it going? / How are you doing?	Great. / Fine. / Good. / Alright. / OK. / Not bad.
	What's up? / What's new?	Nothing. / Not much.

Review

checks students' understanding of the passage.

Language Tips

provides everyday English usage and sentence structure.

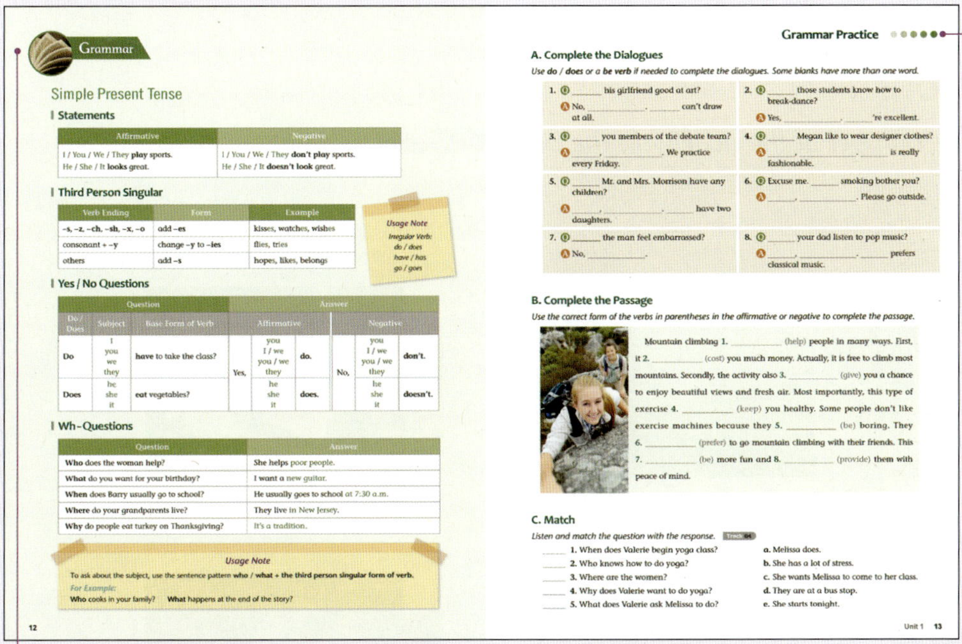

Grammar Practice

enables students to practice grammar in context to enhance accuracy and fluency.

Grammar

presents essential grammar to build overall accuracy.

Reading

enables students to broaden their knowledge through interesting articles.

After You Read

confirms students' understanding of the passage.

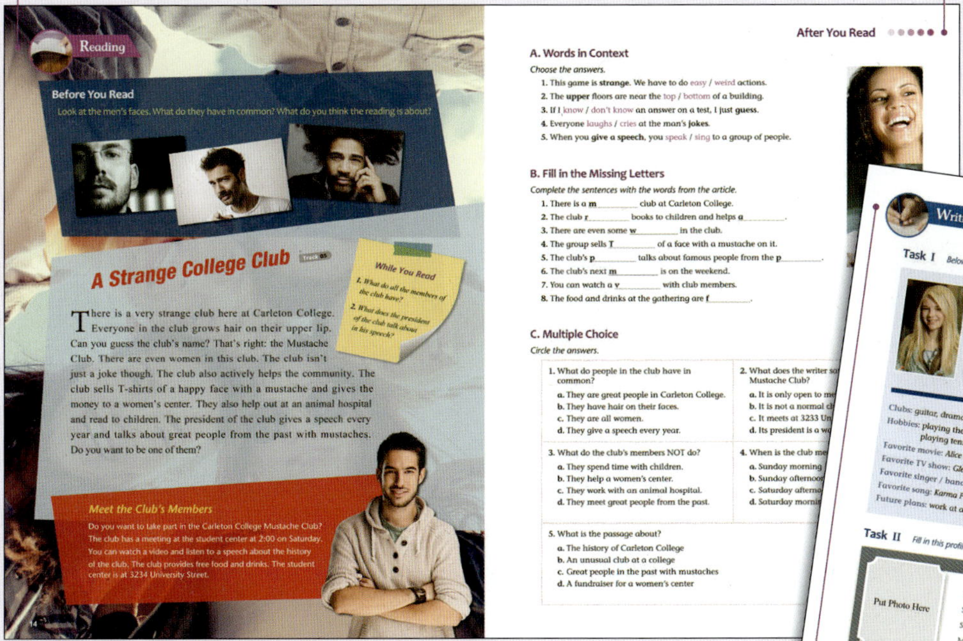

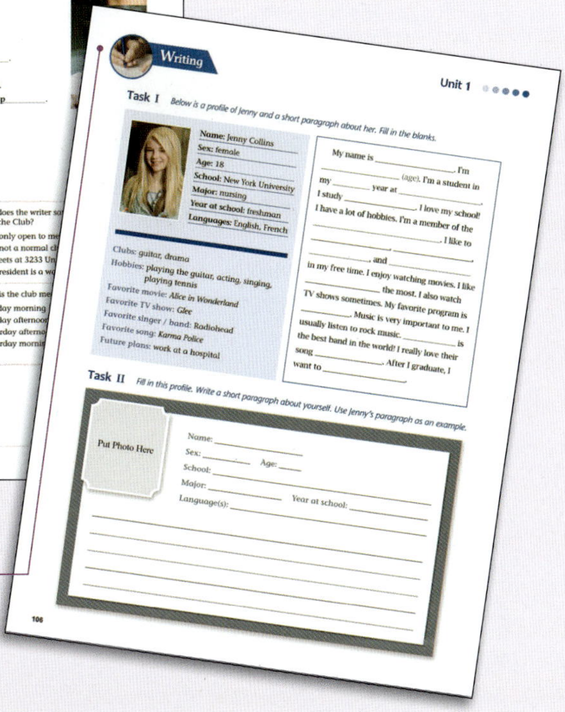

Writing

provides an opportunity for students to practice acquired language in authentic discourse using personalized content.

UNIT 1

Meeting People

1. How did you meet your best friend?
2. What are some good places to meet new people?
3. Are you comfortable talking with people in English?

Words & Expressions

Listen and write the sentence number of the activity in the box. Track 01

School Clubs

basketball

mountain climbing

chess

guitar

in-line skating

break-dancing

1

yoga

drama

swimming

movie

tennis

martial arts

Practice

Practice these sentence patterns using the words above.

- I'm in the ______________ club.
- I want to join the ______________ club.
- I'm a member of the ______________ club.
- I participate in the ______________ club.

Listen Up

Task I *Listen and decide which club is the best for each person.* **Track 02**

Task II *Listen again and choose the answers.*

1. Marie wants to become a break-dancer / hip-hop singer.
2. Doug watches / plays his favorite sport every day.
3. Sharon likes to stay indoors / be in nature.
4. Adam needs to practice in-line skating / skiing.

Act It Out

Practice the conversations with the word choices given.

tennis	guitar	movie	drama
play tennis	play the guitar	watch movies	see plays

1. **A:** Are you in any school clubs?
   B: Yes, I am. I am in the ________________ club.
2. **A:** I belong to the ________________ club.
   B: Cool! I like to ________________ too.
3. **A:** My favorite hobby is to ________________.
   B: Then why don't you join the ________________ club?

Did You Know...?

Place the words from ***Words & Expressions*** *in the correct columns.*

do	play	go	others
			break-dance act watch movies

Conversation

Good to Meet You

Listen and fill in the blanks with the word choices given. Track 03

meet	chess	good	too	pleasure	friendly

Nick and Laura meet for the first time.

Nick: Hi. My name is Nick. Pleased to meet you.

Laura: I'm Laura. Nice to meet you 1. ________. Are you a newcomer to this university?

Nick: Yes, I am. This is my first year here. How about you?

Laura: I'm also new here. I really like it. Everyone is so 2. ________.

Nick: That's true. I'm in two clubs already. Do you participate in any school clubs?

Laura: Yes, I do. I'm in the 3. ________ club. My brother is the president of the club.

Meet the Coach

Jenna introduces Mark to the new swimming coach.

Jenna: Hey, Mark. How are you doing?

Mark: I'm pretty 4. ________, Jenna. And you?

Jenna: Not bad. Thanks. Do you want to 5. ________ someone?

Mark: Sure. Who?

Jenna: Hold on.

(Jenna leaves the room and comes back in with a man.)

Jenna: This is Mr. Mandt. He's the new coach of our swimming club.

Mark: Hello. It's a 6. ________ to meet you. I'm Mark.

Mr. Mandt: Hi, Mark. You can call me Greg. I hope I can help you improve.

Mark: I'm sure you can. Let's get started!

A. Synonyms

Circle the synonym of the word or phrase in bold in the context of the conversations.

1. **pleased** — **a.** happy — **b.** sad
2. **participate in** — **a.** quit — **b.** take part in
3. **president** — **a.** leader — **b.** teacher
4. **pretty** — **a.** quite — **b.** little
5. **hold on** — **a.** keep — **b.** wait
6. **improve** — **a.** become worse — **b.** become better

B. Fill in the Blanks

*Use the words in bold from **A** to complete the sentences.*

1. This chocolate cake is ______________ good.
2. Do you ______________ any sports?
3. I want to be the student body ______________ next year.
4. ______________ a second. I have to get my coat.
5. Nate always gets high scores on tests. He is ______________ with his grades.
6. I don't swim well. I need to ______________ my swimming technique.

C. You Might Also Say...

Write the sentence from the conversations with the same meaning.

1. Are you new at this college?
   = ____
2. And yourself?
   = ____
3. Are you signed up for any school clubs?
   = ____
4. My brother is the club leader.
   = ____
5. My name is Greg.
   = ____

D. Language Tips

Greeting People

	Greeting	Response
Formal	Good morning.	Good morning.
	How are you?	I'm pretty good. How about you?
	Good / Nice / Pleased to meet you.	Good / Nice / Pleased to meet you too.
	It's a pleasure to meet you.	Likewise. / You too.
Informal	How's it going? / How are you doing?	Great. / Fine. / Good. / Alright. / OK. / Not bad.
	What's up? / What's new?	Nothing. / Not much.

Grammar

Simple Present Tense

Statements

Affirmative	Negative
I / You / We / They **play** sports. He / She / It **looks** great.	I / You / We / They **don't play** sports. He / She / It **doesn't look** great.

Third Person Singular

Verb Ending	Form	Example
–s, –z, –**ch**, –**sh**, –x, –o	add –**es**	kisses, watches, wishes
consonant + –**y**	change –**y** to –**ies**	flies, tries
others	add –**s**	hopes, likes, belongs

Usage Note

Irregular Verb:
do / does
have / has
go / goes

Yes / No Questions

Question			Answer					
Do / Does	**Subject**	**Base Form of Verb**	**Affirmative**			**Negative**		
Do	I you we they	**have** to take the class?	Yes,	you I / we you / we they	**do.**	No,	you I / we you / we they	**don't.**
Does	he she it	**eat** vegetables?	Yes,	he she it	**does.**	No,	he she it	**doesn't.**

Wh-Questions

Question	Answer
Who does the woman help?	She helps poor people.
What do you want for your birthday?	I want a new guitar.
When does Barry usually go to school?	He usually goes to school at 7:30 a.m.
Where do your grandparents live?	They live in New Jersey.
Why do people eat turkey on Thanksgiving?	It's a tradition.

Usage Note

To ask about the subject, use the sentence pattern **who** / **what** + **the third person singular form of verb.**

For Example:

Who cooks in your family? **What** happens at the end of the story?

A. Complete the Dialogues

*Use **do** / **does** or a **be verb** if needed to complete the dialogues. Some blanks have more than one word.*

1. Q ______ his girlfriend good at art?
   A No, ____________. ______ can't draw at all.

2. Q ______ those students know how to break-dance?
   A Yes, ____________. ______'re excellent.

3. Q ______ you members of the debate team?
   A ______, ____________. We practice every Friday.

4. Q ______ Megan like to wear designer clothes?
   A ______, ____________. ______ is really fashionable.

5. Q ______ Mr. and Mrs. Morrison have any children?
   A ______, ____________. ______ have two daughters.

6. Q Excuse me. ______ smoking bother you?
   A ______, ____________. Please go outside.

7. Q ______ the man feel embarrassed?
   A No, ____________.

8. Q ______ your dad listen to pop music?
   A ______, ____________. ______ prefers classical music.

B. Complete the Passage

Use the correct form of the verbs in parentheses in the affirmative or negative to complete the passage.

Mountain climbing **1.** __________ (help) people in many ways. First, it **2.** __________ (cost) you much money. Actually, it is free to climb most mountains. Secondly, the activity also **3.** __________ (give) you a chance to enjoy beautiful views and fresh air. Most importantly, this type of exercise **4.** __________ (keep) you healthy. Some people don't like exercise machines because they **5.** __________ (be) boring. They **6.** __________ (prefer) to go mountain climbing with their friends. This **7.** __________ (be) more fun and **8.** __________ (provide) them with peace of mind.

C. Match

Listen and match the question with the response. Track 04

_____ 1. When does Valerie begin yoga class?
_____ 2. Who knows how to do yoga?
_____ 3. Where are the women?
_____ 4. Why does Valerie want to do yoga?
_____ 5. What does Valerie ask Melissa to do?

a. Melissa does.
b. She has a lot of stress.
c. She wants Melissa to come to her class.
d. They are at a bus stop.
e. She starts tonight.

Before You Read

Look at the men's faces. What do they have in common? What do you think the reading is about?

A Strange College Club

Track 05

While You Read

1. What do all the members of the club have?
2. What does the president of the club talk about in his speech?

There is a very strange club here at Carleton College. Everyone in the club grows hair on their upper lip. Can you guess the club's name? That's right: the Mustache Club. There are even women in this club. The club isn't just a joke though. The club also actively helps the community. The club sells T-shirts of a happy face with a mustache and gives the money to a women's center. They also help out at an animal hospital and read to children. The president of the club gives a speech every year and talks about great people from the past with mustaches. Do you want to be one of them?

Meet the Club's Members

Do you want to take part in the Carleton College Mustache Club? The club has a meeting at the student center at 2:00 on Saturday. You can watch a video and listen to a speech about the history of the club. The club provides free food and drinks. The student center is at 3234 University Street.

A. Words in Context

Choose the answers.

1. This game is **strange**. We have to do easy / weird actions.
2. The **upper** floors are near the top / bottom of a building.
3. If I know / don't know an answer on a test, I just **guess**.
4. Everyone laughs / cries at the man's **jokes**.
5. When you **give a speech**, you speak / sing to a group of people.

B. Fill in the Missing Letters

Complete the sentences with the words from the article.

1. There is a **m**__________ club at Carleton College.
2. The club **r**__________ books to children and helps **a**__________.
3. There are even some **w**__________ in the club.
4. The group sells **T**__________ of a face with a mustache on it.
5. The club's **p**__________ talks about famous people from the **p**__________.
6. The club's next **m**__________ is on the weekend.
7. You can watch a **v**__________ with club members.
8. The food and drinks at the gathering are **f**__________.

C. Multiple Choice

Circle the answers.

1. What do people in the club have in common?

a. They are great people in Carleton College.
b. They have hair on their faces.
c. They are all women.
d. They give a speech every year.

2. What does the writer say about the Mustache Club?

a. It is only open to men.
b. It is not a normal club.
c. It meets at 3233 University Street.
d. Its president is a woman.

3. What do the club's members NOT do?

a. They spend time with children.
b. They help a women's center.
c. They work with an animal hospital.
d. They meet great people from the past.

4. When is the club meeting?

a. Sunday morning
b. Sunday afternoon
c. Saturday afternoon
d. Saturday morning

5. What is the passage about?

a. The history of Carleton College
b. An unusual club at a college
c. Great people in the past with mustaches
d. A fundraiser for a women's center

UNIT 2

Time to Eat

1. What's your favorite food?
2. Do you have a healthy diet?
3. Can you draw a food pyramid?

Words & Expressions

Task I *Listen and write the words in the blanks.* Track 06

beef	rice	cereal	pork	mangoes	broccoli	carrots
cheese	yogurt	pears	onions	chicken	corn oil	potatoes

Task II *Write the words from **Task I** to match the pictures.*

Practice

Talk to a partner.

- Do you eat foods from the six groups every day?
- What foods from the list do you like to eat?
- Which fruits do you eat? How about vegetables?
- Do you eat meat? What is your favorite kind of meat?

Listen Up

Task I *Listen and choose the correct shopping list.* Track 07

☐ List A	☐ List B	☐ List C
pineapples	beef	yogurt
beef	yogurt	chicken
yogurt	potatoes	potatoes
potatoes	onions	kiwis
carrots	kiwis	broccoli
kiwis	broccoli	pears
broccoli	oranges	rice
oranges	pears	onions
rice	apples	noodles

Task II *Listen again and fill in the blanks with the words you hear.*

1. Vince plans to ______________ dinner for his ______________.

2. Vince's girlfriend likes to eat ______________, especially ______________.

3. The main dish is beef with ______________. There is also a yogurt and ______________ sauce.

4. Laura wants to cook some ______________, but Vince decides to cook ______________.

5. Vince uses ______________ to make salad for ______________.

Act It Out

Practice the conversations with the word choices given.

meat / vegetables / seafood

pork / beef / lamb / green beans / broccoli / fish / shrimp

breakfast / lunch / dinner

egg sandwiches / potato salad / beef noodle soup / rice with pork

1. A: Do you eat ______________?

B: Yes, I do. I especially like ______________.

2. A: What do you eat for ______________?

B: I usually eat ______________.

3. A: Do you cook at home?

B: Yes. I like to cook / make ______________.

Did You Know...?

We can add ***–y*** *to certain nouns to make adjectives to describe food.*

Noun	Adjective	Noun	Adjective
taste	tasty	salt	salty
oil	oily	health	healthy
juice	juicy	cream	creamy

Fill in the blanks with the appropriate words.

1. This sauce is too ______________. It can make you fat.

2. I don't often eat fried food. It's very ______________.

3. This orange is sweet and ______________.

4. The popcorn is ______________. Have some water with it.

Conversation

Enjoy Free Food

Listen and fill in the blanks with the word choices given. Track 08

much	beef	left	beer	believe	steak

Jill and Rick are talking at a party.

Jill: What's up, Rick? What do you think about these burgers?

Rick: They're pretty good. Most of the food at this party is excellent. Have a 1. _________. They're great!

Jill: You like 2. _________ a lot. You have two burgers and a steak on your plate.

Rick: I'm a huge beef eater.

Jill: I don't eat 3. _________ beef. I prefer fruit. I'm crazy about mangoes. I eat two or three mangoes every day.

Rick: Mangoes are OK.

Jill: Fruit is good for you, but beef is not very healthy.

Rick: Beer is not healthy either. Should I put down my bottle?

Jill: No, not at all. Have a few more bottles of 4. _________. It's free.

Rick: The mangoes are free too. Eat up.

Jill: Good idea. There are some more mangoes in the kitchen, right?

Rick: I 5. _________ so. But can we go in the kitchen?

Jill: I guess so. Let's hurry. There isn't a lot of food 6. _________. Meet me at the bar in 15 minutes.

A. Word Definitions

Replace the words in italics with the choices given. Change the word form if necessary.

excellent	huge	prefer	healthy	hurry

1. Fruit and vegetables are *good for your body*.
   ▶ ____________________
2. The writer's new book is a *big* success.
   ▶ ____________________
3. I need to *go faster*. I'm late for school.
   ▶ ____________________
4. She *likes* black coffee *better*. She doesn't like to add milk or sugar.
   ▶ ____________________
5. This pizza is *delicious*. You're a good cook.
   ▶ ____________________

B. Meanings in Context

Choose the meaning of the sentence in the conversation.

1. I'm a huge beef eater.
a. I eat a lot of beef.
b. I'm big, and I eat beef too.

2. I'm crazy about mangoes.
a. I love to eat mangoes.
b. I feel strange when I eat mangoes.

3. Mangoes are OK.
a. I don't like mangoes.
b. They taste fine.

4. No, not at all.
a. Absolutely not.
b. Of course.

5. It's free.
a. There's nothing to do.
b. There's no cost.

6. Eat up.
a. Eat more.
b. Go upstairs to eat.

C. Language Tips

Asking about a Meal

Greeting
What do you think about / of the . . .? How do you like the . . .? How is / are the . . .? Is / Are the . . . OK?

Response	
It's / They're	excellent / great. ☺ delicious / tasty. pretty good. alright / OK. not very good. terrible. ☹

Practice the sentence patterns using the choices given.

onion rings	cheeseburgers	strawberry yogurt	baked potatoes	fried rice
spaghetti	chicken soup	chocolate cake	fruit juice	pizza

Grammar

Count Nouns vs. Non-Count Nouns

Differences

	Count Nouns			Non-Count Nouns			
Definition	has a singular and plural form			only has a singular form			
Example	a potato two students	an onion four pears	one bottle five mangoes	salt time	news meat	music milk	cheese water

Plural Count Nouns

	Noun Ending	Plural Form	Example	
Regular Plurals	–s, –sh, –ch, –x, –z	add –es	buses	watches
	consonant + –y	change –y to –ies	babies	parties
	–o	add –es or –s	tomatoes	photos
	others	add –s	houses	drivers
Irregular Plurals	wife → wives child → children	man → men foot → feet	person → people mouse → mice	

Articles, Determiners & Quantifiers

Count Nouns	Non-Count Nouns
Do you want a sandwich? They have one daughter.	X
The mangoes are free.	The meat is fresh.
This / That coat is warm.	This / That soup is cold.
These / Those people are my friends.	X
I need to buy some apples.	I need to buy some medicine.
Are there any questions?	Is there any water in the bottle?
We don't have enough chairs for everyone.	I don't have enough money for a new car.
There are a lot of / lots of people at the party.	There is a lot of / lots of food left.
I don't eat many vegetables. (a large amount)	I don't eat much beef. (a large amount)
There are a few books in my bag. (a small amount)	I only want a little milk in my coffee. (a small amount)
Few people use film cameras. (a very small amount)	We have little information on this topic. (a very small amount)

A. Complete the Passage

*Use the correct articles (**a**, **an**, or **the**) to complete the passage. Put an **X** if no word is needed.*

The garden salad is **1.** ________ popular dish in this restaurant. People enjoy **2.** ________ dish because it's delicious. **3.** ________ garden salad is really big. Each plate has **4.** ________ lettuce, **5.** ________ egg, and **6.** ________ tomato. **7.** ________ dressing is good. You can choose **8.** ________ French kind or **9.** ________ Thousand Island. Don't forget to ask for **10.** ________ restaurant's famous blue cheese. It's nice on top of **11.** ________ salad.

B. Fill in the Blanks

*Use **a few**, **a little**, **many**, **much** and the correct form of the words given to complete the sentences.*

mistake	soap	church	friend	time	money	child

1. Let's hurry. There isn't ____________ left. The train leaves in five minutes.
2. There are ____________ in Rome. It's impossible to visit them all in one day.
3. I only have ____________. I can't pay for lunch.
4. Jessica is not very sociable. She only has ____________ at school.
5. This is terrible! I can see ____________ on your math test.
6. Don't put too ____________ in the water.
7. The Jones have ____________. They have a total of seven.

C. Correct the Mistakes

Fix the errors in the dialogue.

Harry: Do you want to go to (a) basketball game?
Marvin: That sounds great, but I need to go shopping.
Harry: Shopping? Really? But you are the huge basketball fan.
Marvin: You're right, but my girlfriend's birthday is tomorrow. I want to cook the dinner for her.
Harry: You're an nice boyfriend. What does she like?
Marvin: I don't know. Do you have many suggestions?
Harry: Cook some seafood pastas. It's a easy dish to make.
Marvin: That's good idea. I can put in a shrimp, just a few white sauce, and any noodles.
Harry: Mmm. She's the lucky girl.

Before You Read

Look at the pictures. Which foods do you often eat? Do you think you have a healthy diet?

Eat More and Lose Weight

Track 09

Are you sick of dieting to lose weight? Good news! Michel Montignac is a food writer and author of *The French Diet*. He says the type of food is more important than the amount of food. He divides all food into two groups, good and bad. It sounds easy, right? You don't even need to exercise too much! The good foods, like vegetables, cereals, and pasta, release sugar into the blood more slowly. They also stop the body from keeping fat. Potatoes, candy, and white flour are examples of bad foods. Try to avoid these foods. Not everyone agrees, but it is a very interesting idea, especially for food lovers who want to stay slim.

While You Read

1. What does The French Diet tell readers?
2. What foods are good for you? What foods should you avoid?

Tips for Healthy Dieting

1. Don't eat too much. Eat until you're 80 percent full.
2. Treat vegetables as the main meal and meat as a side dish.
3. Eat lots of fresh food.
4. Enjoy your meal slowly and use it as a social time.

A. Multiple Choice

Circle the answers.

1. Who is Michel Montignac?
   - **a.** A doctor at a hospital
   - **b.** A food writer
   - **c.** A food lover
   - **d.** A famous French cook

2. Which of these is good food?
   - **a.** Potatoes
   - **b.** White flour
   - **c.** Cereals
   - **d.** Candy

3. Why does Michel Montignac say that vegetables are healthy?
   - **a.** They have a lot of sugar.
   - **b.** They don't let the body store fat.
   - **c.** They are a main meal.
   - **d.** They don't release sugar into the blood.

4. Which is NOT a tip for healthy dieting?
   - **a.** Stop eating before you're full.
   - **b.** Make your meals a pleasant time.
   - **c.** Eat lots of vegetables. Don't eat too much meat.
   - **d.** Do not exercise much.

B. Words with Different Meanings

Match the word in bold with its definition.

1 Jenny and Leo are **sick** of seeing each other. They are not friends anymore. ______
Joe is really **sick**. We should visit him in the hospital. ______
Definition: ⓐ *adj.* not healthy ⓑ *adj.* bored, tired

2 You don't need to **diet**. You're already very slim. ______
I want a **diet** Coke with my burger. ______
Definition: ⓐ *adj.* having low fat or sugar content ⓑ *v.* to eat less to lose weight

3 I **exercise** at the gym three times a week. ______
Swimming can help you **exercise** your arm and leg muscles. ______
Definition: ⓐ *v.* to do sports activities ⓑ *v.* to train a body part

4 If you're already **full**, you can take these cookies home. ______
This train is **full**. We have to wait for the next one. ______
Definition: ⓐ *adj.* having no space ⓑ *adj.* having eaten enough food

C. Choose the Right Tip

Read and write the correct number from tips for healthy dieting.

1. Vegetables are a big part of Greek people's everyday diet. ______
2. Portuguese people like to eat their meals with friends and family. ______
3. In Indonesia, people don't like to eat canned foods. ______
4. Japanese meals are usually smaller in size than Western meals. ______
5. Some restaurants in Italy grow their own vegetables to offer fresh food. ______

UNIT 3 Living with Technology

Words & Expressions

Listen and write the sentence number of the item in the box. Track 10

Electronics and the Internet

a camera

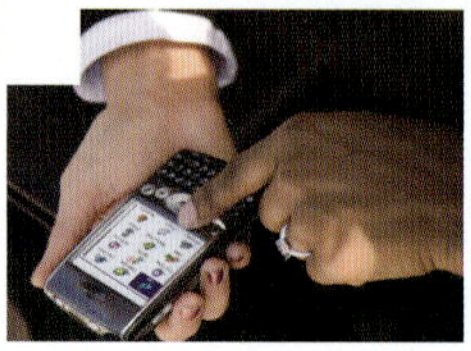
a touch screen phone

an e-mail

a text message

Facebook

MSN messenger

an MP3 player

YouTube

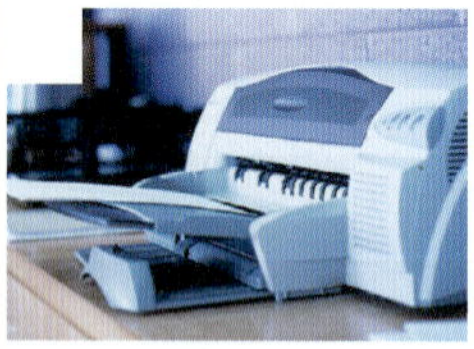
a printer

a copy machine

a laptop computer

the Internet

Match the verbs / verbal phrases with the nouns above. There may be more than one match.

listen to music on	type on	send	use
take pictures with	post on	chat on	surf

Practice

Practice these sentence patterns using the words above.

- Do you know how to ______________?
- It's fun to ______________.
- You can ______________ and talk to your friends.
- I ______________ every day.
- The ______________ doesn't work. I can't ______________.

1. What websites do you visit every day?
2. How has technology changed since you were young?
3. Which technology companies do you trust?

Listen Up

Task I *Listen and check the thing that is being talked about.* **Track 11**

Dialogue 1	Dialogue 2	Dialogue 3	Dialogue 4
☐ Facebook	☐ e-mail	☐ printer	☐ touch screen phone
☐ YouTube	☐ text message	☐ MP3 player	☐ laptop computer

Task II *Listen again and complete the sentences with the words you hear.*

1. Brad has his ____________ from Saturday's ____________ on the Internet.

2. Marvin needs the ______________ for ______________ class.

3. David can buy some ______________ for Matt.

4. Jenny has to ______________ up her ______________.

Act It Out

Practice the conversations with the expressions.

How often do you . . .
go online?
play video games?
check your e-mail?
watch videos on YouTube?
post pictures on Facebook?
look up information on Wikipedia?

Response
I . . . every day / week / weekend.
I . . . once / twice / three times / four times a day.
I never . . .
I . . . all the time / once in a while.

Did You Know...?

least often				most often
never	seldom rarely	sometimes once in a while	usually often	always all the time

1. Max exercises. (rarely) ▶ ________________________________

2. My father drinks coffee. (usually) ▶ ________________________________

3. Steve meets his friends. (once in a while) ▶ ________________________________

4. It is too late to quit smoking. (never) ▶ ________________________________

5. I use Google to search for things online. (every day) ▶ ________________________________

6. Do you go to the movies? (often) ▶ ________________________________

Conversation

Homework or Video Games?

Listen and fill in the blanks with the word choices given. Track 12

sometimes	anymore	send	losing	seldom	chat

Steve is playing a video game. Sandra comes up to say hello.

Sandra: Hi, Steve. What are you doing? Do you want to meet tonight? We can go to dinner and do homework together.

Steve: Oh no! I am 1. __________ this game! What? Oh. Hi, Sandra. How's it going?

Sandra: You're always playing with your toys. We never talk 2. __________!

Steve: That's not true. We 3. __________ all the time. We are talking right now.

Sandra: You prefer posting on Facebook to meeting your friends.

Steve: I meet my friends 4. __________. I can also see what they are doing on their Facebook page.

Sandra: And what about reading books? You 5. __________ read. You need to do it more often.

Steve: Reading is boring. I prefer video games to reading.

Sandra: Fine. Well, would you like to meet later? I can help you with homework.

Steve: Sorry, I can't. I have to 6. __________ a lot of e-mails tonight.

Sandra: You should send them now! You are behaving like a little boy.

A. Complete the Passage

Use the word choices given to complete the passage.

meet	lose	chat	prefer	post	behave

Do you **1.** __________ on the Internet every day? Do you **2.** __________ on Facebook when you are in class? Do you **3.** __________ surfing the Net to going out? Do you feel sad when you **4.** __________ a game on the computer? Then you have a problem. You should not **5.** __________ like that. Go outside more often. **6.** __________ your friends in a coffee shop or play sports. Who knows? You might enjoy yourself more.

B. Adverbs of Frequency

Fill in the blanks with the words given. More than one answer is possible in some of the sentences.

always	never	all the time	sometimes	seldom	often

Dialogue 1

Brad: How __________ do you buy new clothes, Todd?
Todd: I __________ buy new clothes. They're too expensive.
Brad: Really? So what do you do when your clothes get old?
Todd: __________ my parents buy me new clothes for my birthday.

Dialogue 2

Donna: I love this new TV show. It's called *Big Family*.
Karen: I don't know that show. I __________ watch TV at night.
Donna: I watch TV __________. I love it.
Karen: TV is OK. But I like to chat with my friends. That's __________ fun.

C. Language Tips

Making Suggestions

You / We need to + Verb.	Why don't you / we + Verb?
You / We should + Verb.	Why not + Verb?

Practice stating problems and giving suggestions.

Problem	Suggestion
• The schoolwork is difficult.	• Ask your teacher for help.
• I think I'm sick.	• Go to see a doctor.
• My phone doesn't work.	• Call the phone company.
• I can't find room 102.	• Look at the school map.
• I feel tired.	• Get some sleep.

Grammar

Present Continuous Tense

Statements

Subject	Be Verb	(Not)	Verb + –ing
I	am	(not)	watching the news on TV.
Derek	is	(not)	dancing to the music.
The children	are	(not)	having breakfast.

Questions

Question	Response
Is Mr. Lee having a meeting now?	Yes, he is. / No, he isn't.
Are the dogs sleeping?	Yes, they are. / No, they aren't.
What are you doing?	I'm writing an e-mail to my friend.
Where is Bob's mother going?	She is going to the grocery store.

Verb + –ing

Verb Ending	The –ing Form	Example	
one vowel + one consonant	repeat the consonant, then add **–ing**	running	hitting
one vowel + one consonant + –e	drop **–e**, then add **–ing**	coming	leaving
others	add **–ing**	reading	singing

Usage

We use the **present continuous** to talk about situations below.

now	We are talking right now.
repeated action (often negative)	You're always playing with your toys.
around the present time	Maggie is studying hard for her exams this week.
future events	I'm going out tomorrow.

Common time expressions

now	around the present time	in the near future
(just) now right now at the moment	today this week this month	tomorrow on Saturday next week

A. Complete the Letter

*Write the correct articles tense of the verb. Add a **be verb** if necessary.*

Dear Grandma,

It **1.** ______________ (rain) now, so I have time to write to you. I have to be quiet because Mom **2.** ______________ (sleep). I hear that you are sick. I **3.** ______________ (hope) you feel better.

We **4.** ______________ (have) a great time on our vacation. We **5.** ______________ (stay) in a nice hotel. It has a swimming pool. Tomorrow we **6.** ______________ (go) to an amusement park. I really **7.** ______________ (like) amusement parks. Dad **8.** ______________ (take) lots of pictures with his new camera. See you soon!

Love,

Jennifer

B. Match

Listen and match the question with the response. Track 13

	Question		Response
______	**1.** What is David doing right now?	**a.**	David's grandmother.
______	**2.** Is David watching a cartoon?	**b.**	He is watching TV with his brothers.
______	**3.** Who is the hero fighting?	**c.**	He is fighting some bad guys.
______	**4.** What is Neil doing later?	**d.**	No. He is watching an action movie.
______	**5.** Who is having a birthday party tonight?	**e.**	He is going to the movies.
______	**6.** What is Ted always doing?	**f.**	He is exercising all the time.

C. True or False

*Listen and check **True** of **False**.* Track 14

	True	False
1. They are fixing the cafeteria.	☐	☐
2. The chess club is looking for new members.	☐	☐
3. French club members are selling cookies.	☐	☐
4. The French club is going to Paris this year.	☐	☐
5. The football team is playing on Friday.	☐	☐
6. Buses for the football game are leaving at 4:00.	☐	☐
7. The Bible club is collecting old books for Ethiopia.	☐	☐
8. Mr. Vickers is getting married today.	☐	☐

Reading

Before You Read

Who are these people? Do you ever watch their videos? Where can you watch them?

It's a YouTube World

Track 15

While You Read

1. What country is Justin Bieber from?

2. Why does the writer call YouTube a "video universe?"

In 2005, three friends: Steve Chen, Chad Hurley, and Jawad Karim created YouTube. Today, it is the biggest video website in the world. Anybody can post videos on it and have an opportunity to become famous. Justin Bieber is a great example. He was a regular teenager from a poor family in Canada. In 2008, his mother put his singing video on YouTube. A producer saw it and he really liked it. He decided to help Justin record an album. Now, Justin Bieber is a superstar thanks to YouTube. The site lets people visit places far away. They can sit at home and watch a video of an African dance group or a Brazilian soccer player. YouTube is more than just a website. It's a video universe!

Interesting Facts about YouTube

- Justin Bieber's *Baby* has 402,051,105 views on YouTube around the world.
- 70 percent of users come from outside the U.S.
- You would need more than 1,000 years to watch all the videos on YouTube.

A. Word Definitions

Use the clues to fill in the blanks with the word choices given.

create	post	opportunity	famous	teenager	decide	album	superstar

1. My cousin knows a lot about the Internet. He can even ___________ a website. (make)
2. He is the most ___________ movie star in Canada right now. (known about by many people)
3. Joe needs to buy Jessica a gift. Can you help him ___________ what to get? (make a choice)
4. My brother is a little younger than me. He's a(n) ___________. (someone between 13 and 19 years old)
5. Mary loves Lady Gaga. She wants to buy her latest ___________. (music CD)
6. Can you ___________ the pictures from the wedding on Facebook? (put online)
7. I am meeting Kate for coffee. It's a great ___________ to ask her out. (chance)
8. This girl has a lot of talent. She could become a(n) ___________. (very popular person)

B. Words in Context

Choose the answers.

1. Anna is a classmate and good / bad friend. I **like** everyone in my class, including her.
2. He is like / not like everyone else. He's a **regular** person.
3. The **producer** directs / sings the production of the music album.
4. Justin is **recording** some songs / programs in the studio. He has a nice voice.
5. Jim is a happy / sad person **thanks to** his wife. She always supports him.

C. Multiple Choice

Circle the answers.

1. Why did a producer help Justin Bieber become famous?
   a. Because Justin's mother asked him to help.
   b. Because he liked Justin's singing on a YouTube video.
   c. Because he lived in the same neighborhood.
   d. Because Justin was already a superstar.

2. What does Justin Bieber's success prove?
   a. He is a very poor teenager from Canada.
   b. His mother thought he is poor at singing.
   c. Regular people can become famous thanks to YouTube.
   d. YouTube is the biggest website in the world.

3. Who can post videos on YouTube?
   a. Any person
   b. Justin Bieber
   c. African dance groups
   d. All the answers are correct.

4. What is NOT true about YouTube?
   a. Anybody can become famous through YouTube.
   b. Only managers can post videos on YouTube.
   c. People can watch videos from far away places.
   d. People can watch the worldwide news at home.

UNIT 4

Looking Good

1. Can you name some beautiful people?
2. Do you want to look younger or older?
3. What is the first thing you notice about a person?

Words & Expressions

Listen and fill in the blanks with the descriptive adjectives below. Track 16

straight	slender	chubby	blonde	beautiful	dark
bald	curly	young	fit	short	slim

Physical Appearance

Photo 1

The **1.** ______________ girl is an actress. She has long **2.** ______________ hair. Her hair is **3.** ______________, not curly. She has **4.** ______________ blue eyes. She is **5.**______________.

Photo 2

The man doesn't have hair; he is **6.** ______________. He has **7.** __________ eyes. He is not fat; he is strong and **8.** __________. He is old, but he still plays tennis.

Photo 3

This guy is not tall; he's **9.** ______________. He's also **10.** ______________ because he rarely exercises. His eyes and hair are brown.

Photo 4

The woman has **11.** __________ hair. It is long and brown. She likes to exercise, so she is very **12.** __________.

Practice

Put the descriptive adjectives from above in the appropriate columns.

Height	Build	Hair	Eyes	Age

Listen Up

Task I *Listen and circle the correct pictures.* Track 17

Meet Sam's Family

Grandfather	Mother	Sister
a 	a 	a 
b 	b 	b 

Task II *Listen again and fill in the blanks with the words you hear.*

1. Sam's grandfather has gray ______________. He isn't ______________.
2. Sam's mother is tall and ______________. She also has long ______________ hair.
3. Sam has a(n) ___________ sister. Her eyes are ___________, and her hair is long and ___________.

Act It Out

Bring a photo of a member of your family. Practice conversation using the word choices given.

grandma   grandpa   mom   dad   (elder / younger) brother
(elder / younger) sister   cousin   short   tall   cute   slender
chubby   good-looking   curly hair   a beard   dark skin   black eyes

1. Is this your ______________?
2. What's his / her name?
3. Is he / she a ______________ person?
4. Does your ______________ have ______________?

Did You Know...?

Can you guess which sentence is more polite?	Polite	Impolite
1. There's Holly. She's **slender**.	☐	☐
Wow! Holly is so **skinny**.	☐	☐
2. John and I are in the same class. He's **fat**.	☐	☐
My classmate John is a little **chubby** / **overweight**.	☐	☐

Conversation

A Trip Home

Listen and fill in the blanks with the word choices given. Track 18

straight	country	chance	overweight	work	accountant

Liza and Jared talk outside the classroom.

Liza: Hey, Jared. What's up?

Jared: I flew home last weekend. It was a great trip.

Liza: You went back to your home **1.** __________? No way! I forget. Where are you from again?

Jared: I'm from New Zealand. I don't get to see my family often.

Liza: Then you were lucky to spend time with them. What do they look like?

Jared: My dad is tall, bald, and a little **2.** __________. My mom is slender, with **3.** __________ black hair. She's really beautiful. My younger sister, Jill, is chubby and cute.

Liza: I want to meet them sometime! What do your mom and dad do for **4.** __________?

Jared: My mother is a(n) **5.** __________. She loves working with numbers. My father is a computer engineer. He finds electronics interesting.

Liza: Cool. I'm happy that you got the **6.** __________ to return home.

Jared: Thanks. I miss my family already even though I love college.

A. Antonyms

Match the word in bold with its antonym.

lucky •	• thin
spend •	• chubby
tall •	• curly
overweight •	• unfortunate
slender •	• short
straight •	• dull
interesting •	• save

B. Fill in the Blanks

Use the correct form of the words in bold from ***A*** *to complete the sentences.*

1. I ______________ my summer in Bali. I had a really good time.

2. My brother's hair isn't curly. It's ______________.

3. Ted wasn't ______________. He missed his train.

4. My dog is ______________ , now she needs to go on a diet.

5. Ed's new job sounds ______________. He meets many people from different countries.

C. Meanings in Context

Choose the meaning of the sentence in the conversation.

1. No way!

a. That's too bad!
b. That's great!

2. I don't get to see my family often.

a. I don't usually have many opportunities to see my family.
b. I don't like to see my family often.

3. He finds electronics interesting.

a. He looks for interesting electronics.
b. He enjoys learning about electronics.

4. I miss my family already even though I love college.

a. I think of my family a lot.
b. I forgot about my family.

D. Language Tips

Countries and Nationalities

Question		
Where are you from?	Where do you come from?	What's your nationality?
Response		
I'm from . . . / I come from . . .	I'm a(n) . . . / I'm . . .	I was born in . . .

Country	Nationality	Country	Nationality
The U.S. / America	American	The U.K. / England	Briton
Germany	German	Netherlands	Dutch
France	French	Turkey	Turkish

Grammar

Simple Past Tense

Be Verbs

Statements

Subject	Past Tense of Be Verb	Sentence
I / He / She / It	was / was not (wasn't)	the winner of the race.
We / You / They	were / were not (weren't)	happy for the news.

Questions

Question	Response
Was Jessica the best player on the team?	Yes, she was. / No, she wasn't.
Why were Bob and his friend late to the party?	Because they were at work.
When was the play?	It was last Saturday.

Verbs

Verb Ending	Simple Past Form	Example	
–**e**	add –**d**	lived	arrived
one vowel + one consonant	repeat the consonant, then add –**ed**	stopped	begged
consonant + –**y**	change –**y** to –**ied**	tried	carried
others	add –**ed**	enjoyed	worked

Statements

Affirmative	Negative
I flew home last weekend. Kelly threw the ball to her dog. They lived in Los Angeles two years ago.	It didn't rain yesterday morning. Jamal didn't buy the expensive watch. My friends didn't like this band before.

Questions

Question	Answer
Did your brothers go to the gym this morning?	Yes, they did. / No, they didn't.
What did Iris buy yesterday?	She bought a beautiful necklace.
Who drank the milk on the table?	Molly did.

A. Complete the Passage

Use the correct form of the verbs in parentheses to complete the passage.

Travel Journal

My trip to Hawaii **1.** ________ (be) great. I **2.** ________ (go) for a week last summer. We **3.** ________ (fly) from San Francisco to Honolulu. Our plane **4.** ________ (arrive) in the afternoon. We **5.** ________ (sleep) for a few hours at the hotel first. Then we **6.** ________ (watch) the sunset on the beach. The pictures from that day **7.** ________ (be) now on my bedroom wall. The next day, I **8.** ________ (swim) in the ocean. Turtles **9.** ________ (be) all around me. A few days later, we **10.** ________ (fish) in the ocean. I **11.** ________ (catch) a big fish. I really **12.** ________ (love) Hawaii. I want to **13.** ________ (spend) another week there next year.

B. Match

Listen and match the question with the response. Track 19

_____ **1.** Was Darren's accident inside the city?

_____ **2.** Where was the hospital?

_____ **3.** When was the accident?

_____ **4.** Whom did Darren want to visit when he got in the accident?

_____ **5.** What body part did Darren get hurt?

_____ **6.** Why did Darren run into the car?

a. He wanted to see his friend Terry.

b. It was last Saturday.

c. It was near Darren's house.

d. He rode too fast, and the car turned in front of him.

e. No. It was outside the city.

f. He hurt his arm.

C. Correct the Mistakes

Fix the errors in the passage.

Many photographers go to Taroko National Park in Taiwan on August fifth every year to take pictures. What makes them go there? A long time ago, a photographer ~~take~~ took a picture there. The photographer's name be Alison Wen. Wen's photo be in black and white, not color. In the photo, you can see the moon near some mountains. It is beautiful and mysterious. It become very popular. People see the picture and go to the same place to take the same picture just like Wen's. Scientists studyed the photo and did say Wen taking the picture of the moon around 7 o'clock in the evening. And every seven years, the moon being in the same place over the mountains.

Reading

Before You Read

Do you think these women are beautiful? What do you think about these women's make up?

Dangerous Beauty

Track 20

While You Read

1. Why did women in Shakespeare's time shave the hair from their front hairlines and eyebrows?

2. What did people of the time think of as "perfect beauty?"

Can you imagine what fashions were like in Shakespeare's time? Believe it or not, pictures from his time show women who don't have eyebrows. They thought a high forehead was attractive and they shaved the hair from their front hairlines and eyebrows. Also many women dyed their hair red. At that time, women followed the style of Queen Elizabeth. Her red hair was a real vogue among women. In addition, a pale complexion was popular then. People thought of pale skin as a sign of nobility and delicacy. They used ceruse to whiten their faces. They applied this white foundation to their neck and chest, too. After making their skin white, they used a variety of reds upon their cheeks and lips. By doing this, women could get perfect beauty.

However the beauty they earned cost them dearly. Ceruse is a mixture of vinegar and lead powder, which is dangerous to their health. The lead poisoned them. Isn't it unbelievable that people would do anything to be beautiful?

A. Synonyms

Match the word in bold with its synonym.

imagine •	• impressive
picture •	• numerous
many •	• guess
dye •	• trend
unbelievable •	• portrait
vogue •	• tint

B. Fill in the Blanks

*Use the words in bold from **A** to complete the sentences. Change the word form if necessary.*

1. Henna likes to draw ___________ of people walking on the street.
2. Old pop music has come back into ___________ after the concert.
3. My sister ___________ her hair green two years ago.
4. I can't ___________ how angry you are.
5. It was ___________ that all the people were gathering at the hall to see him.
6. I have ___________ things to do, but I don't know what to do first.

C. Words with Different Meanings

Match the word in bold with its definition.

1 Her **face** turned red with shame when everyone looked at her. ______
How can I **face** her? We haven't seen each other for years after we fought. ______
Definition: ⓐ *n.* the front part of the head ⓑ *v.* to meet or confront

2 If you want to **apply** for this job, you need a Bachelor's degree in nursing. ______
It is effective to **apply** mayonnaise to your hair as a conditioner. ______
Definition: ⓐ *v.* to spread ⓑ *v.* to request formally

3 Even small amounts of **lead** can cause serious health problems. ______
He can inspire the members and **lead** the team to victory. ______
Definition: ⓐ *n.* a heavy toxic metallic element ⓑ *v.* to guide or control

D. True or False

*Check **True** or **False**.*

	True	False
1. Queen Elizabeth had red hair and most women in her time hated it.	☐	☐
2. Women changed their hair to black during the Elizabethan Era.	☐	☐
3. Women in Shakespeare's time shaved their eyebrows for beauty.	☐	☐
4. Lead is a cosmetic which is good for health.	☐	☐
5. Some women took a lot of risks in order to look beautiful.	☐	☐

UNIT 5

Not Feeling So Good

Words & Expressions

Fill in the blanks using the word choices given.

cough	runny nose	toothache	headache	fever
stomachache	sore throat	neck pain	sleeping problems	

Symptoms

I have a ________________.

I have a ________________.

I have a ________________.

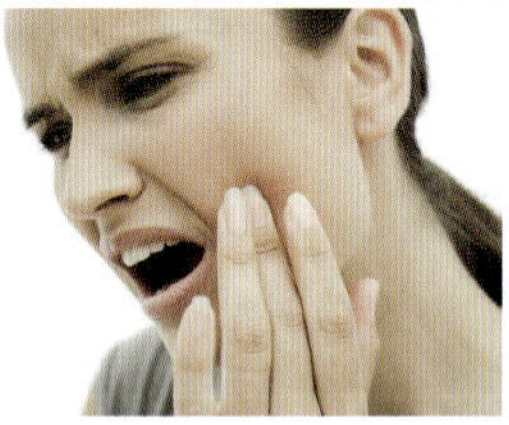

I have a ________________.

I have a ________________.

I have a ________________.

I have a ________________.

I have a ________________.

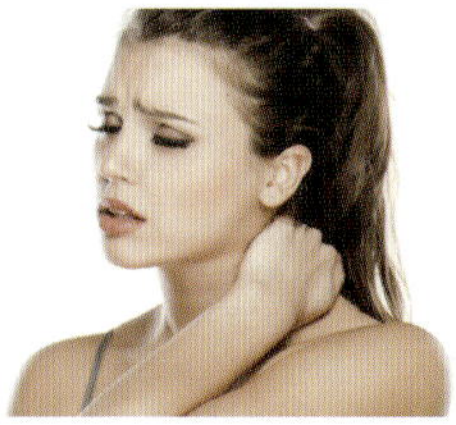

I have a ________________.

Listen and write the correct sentence number in the box. Track 21

Practice

Talk to a partner.

- How often do you go to see a doctor?
- Have you ever had a high fever?
- What do you do to keep healthy?

1. Do you go to see a doctor every time you feel unwell?
2. What foods do you eat when you are sick?

Listen Up

Listen and check ***True*** *or* ***False.*** Track 22

Sally didn't go to work today.	True	False
1. She was out in the rain.	☐	☐
2. Her head hurts.	☐	☐
3. She has a toothache.	☐	☐
4. She thinks she has a stomachache.	☐	☐
5. She needs to rest at home.	☐	☐

Johnny is sick. His dad is very worried.	True	False
1. His stomach hurts a lot.	☐	☐
2. He feels dizzy.	☐	☐
3. He doesn't want any food.	☐	☐
4. He has a high fever.	☐	☐
5. The pain makes him cry.	☐	☐

Act It Out

Practice the conversations with the word choices given.

dizzy	sick	tired	weak	bad
headache	sore throat	neck pain	sore muscles	
head	throat	neck	muscles	

1. A: I feel ___________.

B: Do you have (a) ___________?

A: Yes, I do. My ___________ hurt(s) a lot.

2. A: My ___________ is / are sore.

B: Really? Me too! I also have (a) ___________.

3. A: Would this medicine help my ___________?

B: No, but it can help your ___________.

Did You Know...?

There are different ways to talk about pain.

Words	Sentences	
head ear back tooth stomach	I have a(n) _________ache.	
throat neck feet back muscles	I have (a) sore _________. My _________ is / are hurting.	My _________ is / are sore. My _________ hurt(s).

Conversation

Feeling Sick?

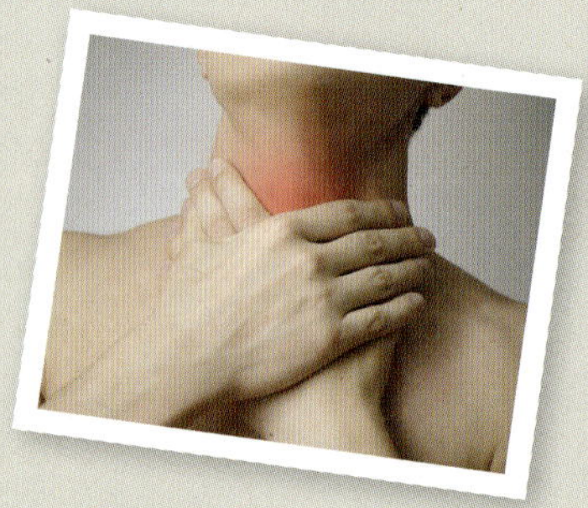

Listen and fill in the blanks with the word choices given. Track 23

sore	deeply	fever	possible	pill	take

Nick is talking to a nurse on the phone.

Nick: Hello. I'd like to see Dr. Chan as soon as **1.** __________.

Nurse: Can I **2.** __________ your name?

Nick: My name's Nicholas Wang.

Nurse: Dr. Chan has time this afternoon. Would you be able to come in at three o'clock?

Nick: That sounds fine. Thanks.

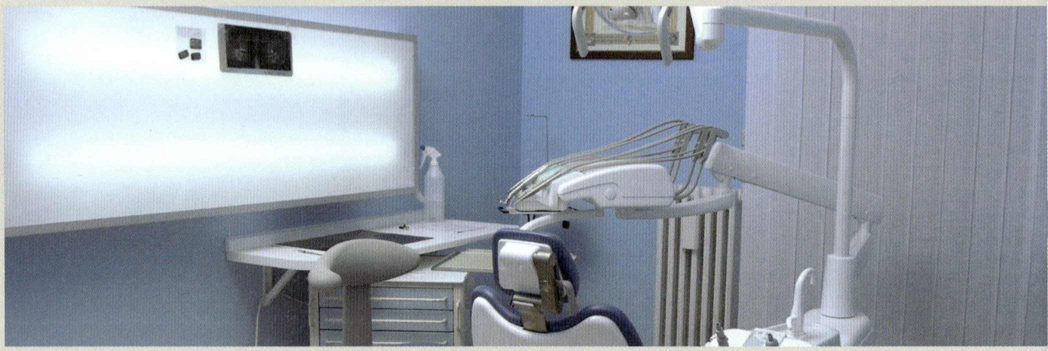

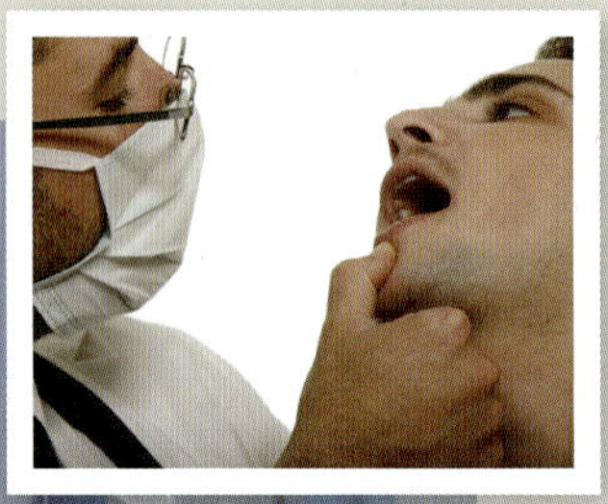

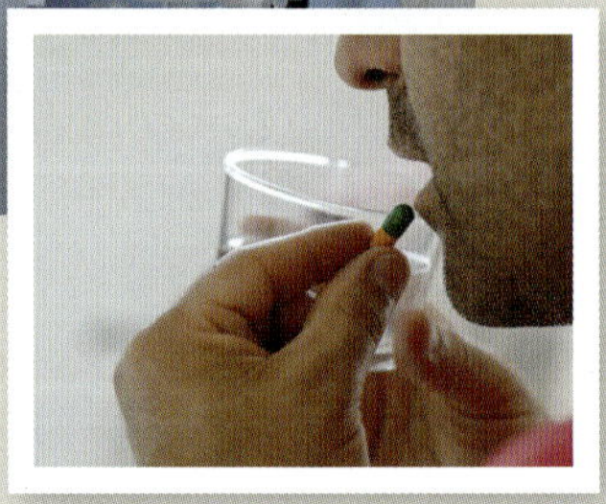

(*Nick enters the doctor's office.*)

Dr. Chan: Hi, Nick. What's the matter?

Nick: I have a high **3.** __________ and a headache.

Dr. Chan: Does your body hurt?

Nick: Yes. My neck hurts, and my muscles are **4.** __________. And I can't stop coughing.

Dr. Chan: When did the pain start?

Nick: I started feeling bad last week. My mom made me take out the garbage. It was cold outside. I was sick a day later.

Dr. Chan: Can I have you take off your shirt? Now breathe **5.** __________. Hmm. It doesn't sound good. Let me check your throat. It looks red. Are you taking any medicine at the moment?

Nick: No.

Dr. Chan: OK. Please take this medicine with food. It can make you feel better. Take one **6.** __________ every six hours and drink lots of water.

Nick: Thank you.

A. Word Definitions

Use the clues to fill in the blanks with the word choices given. Change the word form if necessary.

be able to	fever	take off	breathe	at the moment	lots of

1. Tom ____________ come to my party. He doesn't have to work on that day. (can)
2. I'm not too busy ____________. (right now)
3. Feel Johnny's forehead. He seems to have a ____________. (temperature)
4. The house costs ____________ money. (a large amount of)
5. Air pollution is serious in Beijing. It is hard to ____________ outside. (take air into your lungs)
6. It's warm today. You should ____________ your jacket. (remove)

B. You Might Also Say . . .

Write the sentence from the conversation with the same meaning.

1. I want to see Dr. Chan very soon.
   = ____
2. May I have your name?
   = ____
3. Do you have any pain?
   = ____
4. I keep coughing as well.
   = ____
5. Please don't take this medicine on an empty stomach.
   = ____

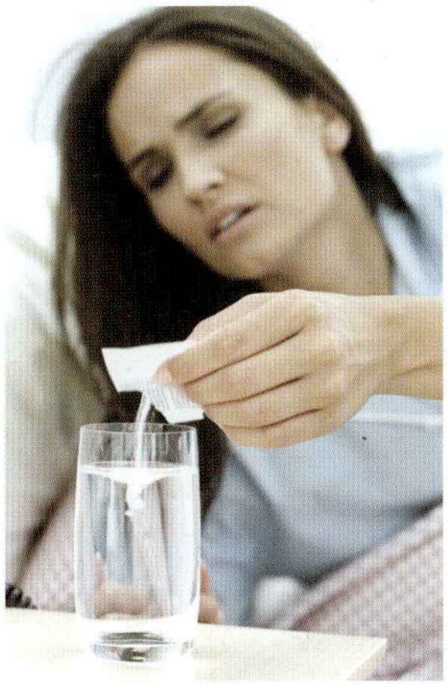

C. Language Tips

Making an Appointment

A Patient Might Say . . .
I'd like to see Dr. (last name) (time). I need to see a doctor (time). Could I come in (time)? Can Dr. (last name) see me (time)? Does Dr. (last name) have time to see me (time)?

A Nurse Might Say . . .
Dr. (last name) has time (time). Would you be able to come in (time)? When would you be available to come in? When would you like to come in? How about (time)? / Is (time) possible?

Practice the sentence patterns using the information given.

The patient is available...	on Wednesday morning	today between 1 and 4	right now
The doctor is available...	at 11 on Tuesday	after two on Friday	today at 2:30

Grammar

Linking Verbs

Definition

Most verbs are action verbs. They tell what the subject does. Some verbs link an adjective or a noun to the subject. We call them **linking verbs.**

be	feel	look	taste	smell	sound
appear	seem	become	grow	turn	remain

Mr. Chan is a good doctor.
I feel sick.
Your throat looks red.

Usage

Some linking verbs can be used in more than one way. Action verbs are usually used with **adverbs,** not **adjectives.**

Example	Verb Usage	Meaning
The noodles tasted good.	linking verb	to have a taste
I tasted the noodles.	action verb	to eat

Example	Verb Usage	Meaning
The leaves turn yellow in fall.	linking verb	to change
The road turns sharply.	action verb	to curve

Causative Verbs

A **causative verb** is used when someone causes something to happen.

Verb	Structure	Meaning
make	make + somebody + Verb	to cause one to do something
have	have + somebody + Verb	to order one to do something
let	let + somebody + Verb	to allow one to do something
get	get + somebody + to Verb	to ask one to do something

My mom made me take out the garbage.
Can I have you take off your shirt?
Let me check your throat.
I got Clara to send you some information.

A. Recognize Linking and Action Verbs

*Decide if the word in bold is a **linking verb** or an **action verb**. Check the box.*

	Sentence	Linking Verb	Action Verb
1	Eddie **looked** at his sister.		
	You **look** tired.		
2	People start to have health problems when they **grow** older.		
	This plant **grows** well in most areas.		
3	The dog **smelled** the food.		
	That white flower **smells** sweet.		
4	The man **sounded** the alarm.		
	Your mother called me. She **sounded** worried.		

B. Words in Context

Choose the answers.

1. The man **turned** the pages of the book slow / slowly.
2. You should try to **remain** calm / calmly during an emergency.
3. When Molly thinks of her grandma, she **becomes** sad / sadly.
4. A man **appeared** sudden / suddenly at my door.
5. This meat **tastes** bad / badly. We should throw it away.
6. I **feel** tired / tiredly. I need to get some rest.
7. Kathy **seems** happy / happily at her new job.
8. My hair **grows** quick / quickly. I need to get a haircut every month.

C. Fill in the Blanks

*Use the words **make**, **have**, **let**, or **get** to complete the sentences. Change the word form if necessary. For some questions, more than one answer is correct.*

1. Can you ____________ your brother to help me?
2. My parents don't ____________ me go out at night.
3. Can you ____________ your secretary send me the letter?
4. Dr. Linda ____________ her students correct their mistakes last class.
5. Please ____________ John to drive me to school.
6. Ben is a funny person. He always ____________ me laugh.
7. ____________ me take a look at your work.
8. Mrs. Kelly ____________ her son clean his room.

Reading

Before You Read

Look at the pictures. When do we need these things? Which one do you think is the most useful?

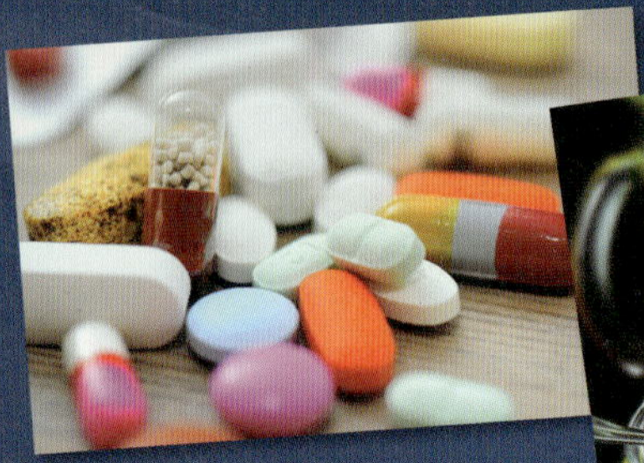

Natural Medicine for Your Cold

Track 24

While You Read

1. How is garlic helpful?

2. What food is good for a runny nose?

3. When should you use honey?

When you get sick, what do you do? Some people go to the drugstore to buy medicine. Some visit the doctor, and some just rest at home.

Some foods can make you feel better when you're sick. Most people know that green tea improves your health when you have a cold. Strawberries help when you have the flu, and honey is good if you have a sore throat.

Did you know that garlic is also effective? Garlic can prevent colds. It also makes them last for a shorter time. Just don't forget to brush your teeth after you eat it!

Hot peppers are also effective. Spicy peppers help stop a runny nose. Of course, you don't need to eat the peppers by themselves. You can mix them with your food.

Chicken soup is another cold remedy. Some doctors started recommending chicken soup as a cold medicine back in the 12th century. The chemicals in chicken soup are similar to those in modern medicine.

The next time you're coughing, sneezing, or fighting a fever, don't go to the drugstore. Try some healthy foods instead!

A. Word Definitions

Use the clues to fill in the blanks with the word choices given. Change the word form if necessary.

natural	drugstore	prevent	effective	flu	sore	recommend	century

1. Drinking green tea could ____________ cancer. (stop)
2. I have a high fever. Maybe I have the ____________. (illness similar to a bad cold)
3. There is a(n) ____________ around the corner. You can buy cold medicine there. (shop selling medicine)
4. It took 97 years – almost a(n) ____________ – to finish the building. (100 years)
5. Tim knows a(n) ____________ way of losing weight. He lost 20 pounds in one week. (successful)
6. This yogurt is completely ____________. It's made from milk and fresh fruit. (not made by people)
7. Laura ran 12 kilometers yesterday. Her legs are really ____________ now. (painful)
8. Seth ____________ this movie to me. I hope it's good. (suggest)

B. Words with Different Meanings

Match the word in bold with its definition.

1 I hurt my ankle, so I need to **rest** for a few weeks. ______
You can have the **rest** of my French fries. I'm full. ______
Definition: ⓐ *n.* what is left ⓑ *v.* to stop activity

2 What's the **last** movie you went to see? ______
Lunar New Year celebrations **last** for 15 days. ______
Definition: ⓐ *adj.* most recent ⓑ *v.* to continue for a period of time

3 The whole country had soccer **fever** during the World Cup. ______
Charles was in bed all day with a high **fever**. ______
Definition: ⓐ *n.* a kind of excitement ⓑ *n.* a high body temperature

C. Complete the Passage

Use the correct form of the words given to complete the passage.

brush	remedy	fight

Bad breath can cause a lot of problems. It might make it difficult for you to find a boyfriend or girlfriend or to advance in your career. There are several kinds of 1. ____________ for bad breath. One is keeping your mouth clean by 2. ____________ your tongue. Another way to 3. ____________ bad breath is to drink lots of water. These solutions not only help bad breath, but they can also make a cold go away.

UNIT 6

The Big Screen

1. What are your favorite movies?
2. Are there any types of movies that you don't like?
3. How often do you go to the movies?

Words & Expressions

Write the movie type under each poster.

a romance movie	a horror movie	a western	a drama
a comedy	a science-fiction movie	an action movie	a cartoon

Types of Movies

Listen and write the sentence number in the box. Track 25

Practice

Talk to a partner.

- What is your favorite movie type?
- What kind of movies don't you like?
- How often do you watch movies?
- Do you prefer to watch movies at a movie theater or at home?

Listen Up

Task I *Listen and check the box.* Track 26

	Statement	*Dead Earth*	*The Bad Cook*
1	The children are unhappy because their parents fight all the time.		
2	The character opens a restaurant.		
3	The character hides from the police.		
4	The husband tries to find his wife.		
5	People got sick after eating at the restaurant.		

Task II *Listen again and fill in the chart.*

Movie	Type	Description	Good Actors?	Good Movie?
Dead Earth	________	silly sad scary bad serious intelligent	☐ Yes ☐ No	☐ Yes ☐ No
The Bad Cook	________	excellent dumb funny boring strange horrible	☐ Yes ☐ No	☐ Yes ☐ No

Act It Out

Practice the conversation with the word choices given.

serious exciting scary romantic
drama(s) action movie(s)
horror movie(s) romance movie(s)
like it too don't like it
never saw it want to see it
actor actress director

1. **A:** I like ____________ movies.
   B: Me too. I prefer to watch ____________.
2. **A:** This is a great movie. It's a(n) ____________.
   B: I ____________.
3. **A:** My favorite ____________ is (*name*).
   B: I agree. I enjoy his / her ____________.

Did You Know...?

see a movie **go to** a movie **go to** the movies **take in** a movie	**star** in a movie **appear** in a movie **be** in a movie	**make** a movie **shoot** a movie

Use the phrases above to complete the sentences. Change the word form if necessary.

1. The director ______________ in Venice, Italy.
2. What are you doing on Friday night? Do you want to ______________?
3. My uncle isn't a famous actor, but he ______________ 20 years ago.

Conversation

Movie Night

Listen and fill in the blanks with the word choices given. Track 27

waiting	comedy	third	angry	forgive	agreed

Jeff and Jordan are waiting by the movie theater. Jessica comes by.

Jeff: Well, Jessica is late.

Jordan: This is the **1.** ________ time this month!

Jeff: She is never on time. We **2.** ________ to meet at half past seven. It's ten to eight now!

Jessica: Guys . . . Hi. I'm late. I'm really sorry.

Jeff: Come on, Jessica. This is not the first time. You came late to John's party on Friday.

Jessica: Please don't be **3.** ________ at me.

Jordan: It's alright. Don't worry about it.

Jessica: Thanks for **4.** ________. The popcorn is my treat tonight.

Jeff: I love popcorn! OK. We **5.** ________ you. I'm excited about this movie!

Jessica: Who's in it?

Jeff: Will Smith and that British girl. I forgot her name.

Jessica: What is it about?

Jeff: It's a(n) **6.** ________ about two friends. I heard it's really funny.

Jordan: The movie opened in the first week of April. All my friends saw it already.

Jeff: The movie starts in five minutes. Jessica, you still have enough time to buy us popcorn and drinks.

Jessica: Drinks too? OK, I guess. Let's go in.

A. Meanings in Context

Choose the meaning of the sentence in the conversation.

1. She is never on time. **a.** She is always late. **b.** She never knows the time.	**2.** Come on, Jessica. **a.** Come over here, Jessica. **b.** Don't make excuses, Jessica.
3. The popcorn is my treat tonight. **a.** I will buy you some popcorn. **b.** The popcorn tastes great tonight.	**4.** The movie opened in the first week of April. **a.** The movie played in theaters for one week in April. **b.** The movie started playing in theaters in April.

B. Word Definitions

Use the clues to fill in the blanks with the word choices given.

agreed	guy	forgive	comedy	funny	enough

1. I'm really sorry. I hope you can ____________ me someday. (not be angry anymore)

2. This is my favorite movie. It's really ____________. (makes people laugh)

3. Jessica and I decided to watch a movie. Tony ____________ to join us for the movie. (say *yes*)

4. Look at that ____________ with a yellow hat and a big dog. (man)

5. I want to buy that book. Do we have ____________ money left? (amount you need)

6. Tom likes to see a(n) ____________. It makes him laugh. (humorous movie)

C. Fill in the Blanks

Use the prepositions in the box to complete the sentences. Some choices can be used more than once.

past	at	by	about	to

1. Could you come _________ my office this afternoon?

2. It's only 11:03. The bus leaves at half _________ eleven.

3. Samuel always comes early _________ class.

4. Tom closed the door violently because he was angry _________ his sister.

5. Don't worry _________ your test. You studied very hard.

6. Karen's son is excited _________ his birthday party.

D. Language Tips

Apologizing

Saying Sorry	Showing Anger	Forgiving
I'm really sorry.	Come on!	It's alright / OK.
Please don't be angry at / with me.	Give me a break!	Don't worry about it.
I apologize.	How could you do this?	We forgive you.
This is my fault.	I can't believe this!	It's not a big deal.

Grammar

Talking about Time

Prepositions

Preposition	Usage		Example	
in	months seasons	years periods of time	in June in (the) winter	in 2025 in the first week of April
on	dates days of the week	holidays	on March 31st on Friday	on Christmas
at	clock time		at 3 p.m.	at half past seven

Questions

Question	Response
When is your vacation?	It is in August.
What day is Halloween?	It is on Thursday.
What time is our train?	It is at 10:20.
What time is it? / What is the time?	It / The time is three o'clock.

Usage Note

We can write dates as regular numbers, but must remember to say them as ordinal numbers (first, second, third, etc.). Use ordinal numbers for streets and the floors of buildings as well.

Telling Time

Use the following phrases to tell time.

0-30 minutes	(*minutes*) **past** / **after** (*hour*)	30 minutes	half **past** (*hour*)
15 minutes	(*a*) quarter **past** / **after** (*hour*)	31-60 minutes	(*minutes*) **to** (*hour*)

	It's seven oh five. It's five (minutes) **past** / **after** seven.		It's seven thirty. It's half **past** seven.
	It's seven fifteen. It's (a) quarter **past** / **after** seven.		It's seven forty-five. It's (a) quarter **to** eight.

A. Correct the Mistakes

Fix the errors in the passage.

My friend Jenny lives on ~~Six~~ Sixth Avenue. Her twenty-first birthday is at two weeks. It's in June 25th. Her birthday is in Monday, but we are having a party in the weekend.

Jenny likes sports very much. She gets up on seven every mornings and exercises. In noon, she eats a healthy lunch with lots of vegetables. She loves to run. She even ran a marathon at 2009. On summer, Jenny and I play tennis in Thursday afternoons. She is really good and beats me most of the time. Last Thursday, however, I beat her!

B. Match

Listen and match the question with the response. Track 28

______	**1.** When does the big sale begin?	**a.** They open at 9 a.m.
______	**2.** What day does the sale end?	**b.** It begins at seven in the evening.
______	**3.** When are women's shoes 50 percent off?	**c.** It starts on November fifth.
______	**4.** Are men's dress pants 40 percent off on Sunday?	**d.** Sunday is the final day.
______	**5.** What time does the toy sale begin?	**e.** They are half price on Thursday.
______	**6.** When do the doors open from Monday to Friday?	**f.** No, but they are on Friday and Saturday.

C. Fill in the Blanks

Listen and write the words you hear to complete the sentences. Track 29

Hamilton Movie House Showtimes

Toy Adventure	3:10 p.m.	5:30 p.m.	7:50 p.m.	midnight
The Biggest Gun	1:00 p.m.	4:25 p.m.	9:45 p.m.	opened on August 18th
Where Am I?	4:30 p.m.	8:45 p.m.	11:35 p.m.	opens on August 22nd

1. Stephen and Carl enjoy going to the movies in __________ to stay out of the __________.
2. The first __________ of *Toy Adventure* is at __________ after __________.
3. Stephen thinks *Toy Adventure* is a movie for __________.
4. The __________ movie *The Biggest Gun* is showing at a(n) __________ to __________, but Carl thinks it's too __________.
5. Today is August __________; *Where Am I?* doesn't __________ until the __________.

Reading

Before You Read

Look at the pictures. Do the animals below remind you of certain movies?

The Wildest Job in Movies

Track 30

While You Read

1. Who is Mark Forbes? What does he do?
2. How many types of animals are in Evan Almighty?
3. Why do animal actors have doubles?

There are dozens of jobs on a movie set, and some of them are a little strange. One of the most unusual jobs belongs to animal coordinators. These workers have to train and control all of the animals in a movie.

Coordinators have to manage more than one animal for a role. Like humans, almost all main animal characters have at least one double. The double must look just like the star. There might be one dog to do tricks, another to stay in one place, and a third to run from one place to another.

The animal coordinator for the movie *Evan Almighty*, Mark Forbes, had a huge challenge. He had to train about 100 types of animals to walk onto a large boat. He filmed many of the animals separately — he didn't want them to run after each other. After careful planning and effort, Forbes and his team managed to work to keep the animals healthy and maintain a safe atmosphere on the set. Managing animals on a movie set is a wild and unusual job. Do you want to try it?

More Unusual Jobs

- Greensmen place plants in film scenes.
- Armorers are responsible for the guns in a movie.

A. Fill in the Blanks

Use the word choices given to complete the sentences. Change the word form if necessary.

set	film	role	character	double	scene

1. Rachel is playing a leading ____________ in the movie.
2. The actor had two ____________ to do the running and fighting for him.
3. The street is closed because people are ____________ a movie.
4. It was a very sad ____________, and the audience began to cry.
5. The main ____________ in the comedy is a young doctor.
6. It took six months to build the ____________ for the movie.

B. Words in Context

Choose the answers.

1. **Dozens of** people bought tickets, so we prepared a few / a lot of chairs.
2. We decided to get a wedding **coordinator** to pay for / plan our wedding day.
3. The final exam was a **challenge**. It was very easy / hard for the students.
4. This set of books is sold **separately**. You can buy them one by one / together.
5. I like the **atmosphere** of my neighborhood. People can live in a safe environment / air.

C. Words with Different Meanings

Match the word in bold with its definition.

1 Ted **managed** his own store for two years. ______
Julia was tired, but she **managed** to finish the race. ______
Definition: ⓐ *v.* to handle or direct ⓑ *v.* to succeed in doing something difficult

2 My brother believes everything, so it's easy to **trick** him. ______
The elephants can do some **tricks**. ______
Definition: ⓐ *n.* a clever act to entertain ⓑ *v.* to fool someone

3 The mayor wants to **maintain** control of the city. The voters get to decide next week. ______
Dan didn't have a job, so his wife had to **maintain** the family. ______
Definition: ⓐ *v.* to support ⓑ *v.* to keep the same condition

D. True or False

*Check **True** or **False**.*

	True	False
1. Mark Forbes had to train animals to run after each other.	☐	☐
2. There were around 100 types of animals in *Evan Almighty*.	☐	☐
3. Mark Forbes filmed animals for *Evan Almighty* one by one.	☐	☐
4. In a movie with animals, a double looks just like another animal.	☐	☐
5. A safe atmosphere is important when animals are on the set.	☐	☐

UNIT 7

How Do You Feel?

1. Do you usually feel good when you wake up?
2. What emotions have you felt today?
3. Do animals have emotions?

Words & Expressions

Listen and write the sentence number of the feeling in the box. Track 31

Feelings

happy

lonely

sad

proud

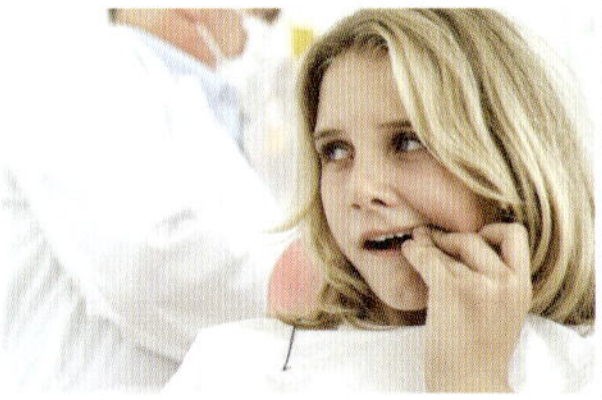

nervous

down

calm

mad

jealous

comfortable

curious

afraid

Practice

Talk to a partner. What makes you feel a certain way?

- ____________________ puts me in a good mood.
- ____________________ makes me feel sad.
- I get nervous when ____________________.
- ____________________ makes me feel comfortable.

Listen Up

Task I *Listen and fill in the blanks with the words from **Words & Expressions**.* Track 32

1. Lucy is ____________. She was accepted by a university in London.

2. Stacey is ____________. James didn't call her today.

3. Jeff is ____________. He didn't study at all.

4. Alex is ____________. He thinks Barbara is lying to him.

Task II *Listen again and check **True** or **False**.*

	True	False
1. Lucy wants to study physics in London.	☐	☐
2. Lucy got a phone call from a school in England.	☐	☐
3. Stacey thinks James likes her a lot.	☐	☐
4. Jeff didn't study much for the exam.	☐	☐
5. Alex doesn't believe Barbara.	☐	☐

Act It Out

Practice the conversations with the word choices given. Change the word form if necessary.

exam	interview	baseball game	speech	
happy	glad	sad	down	
get a good grade		pass the driving test	receive bad news	fail the class

1. A: How was the ________________?

B: It was good. I'm ________________. / It was terrible. I feel ________________.

2. A: Did you ________________?

B: Yes, I did. / No, I didn't. I'm very ________________.

3. A: Did something happen? You look ________________.

B: Yeah, you're right. I'm really ________________. I ________________.

Did You Know...?

Fill in the blanks with the prepositions below. Some choices can be used more than once.

for	of	about	at

1. I'm afraid ________ cockroaches.

2. Susan is nervous ________ the speech.

3. I'm really happy ________ Sam. He's getting married.

4. The woman is proud ________ her children.

5. The people are mad ________ the president.

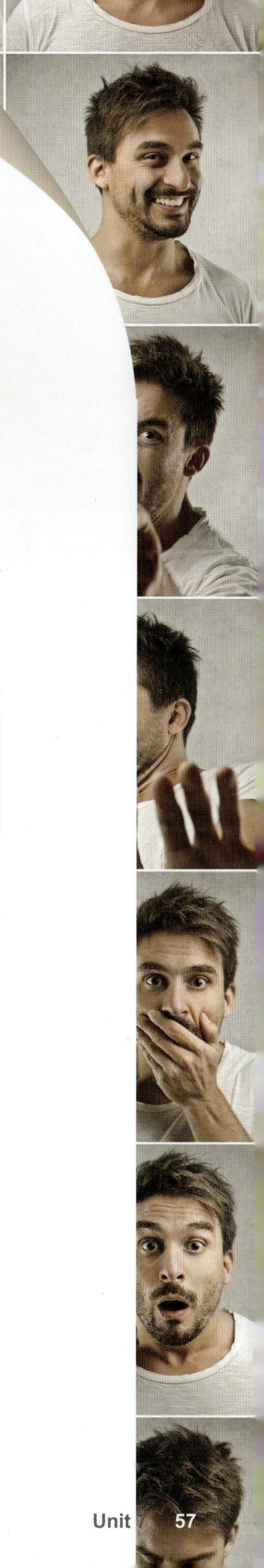

Conversation

Bad News, Good News

Listen and fill in the blanks with the word choices given. Track 33

bored	happened	better	marry	down	shocked

Jennifer and Stan meet for dinner.

Jennifer: Hey, Stan. Is everything OK? You look a little 1. __________.

Stan: Everything is fine.

Jennifer: Look. We're friends. You can tell me. You shouldn't feel embarrassed about anything.

Stan: I guess you're right. Alright. Ashley broke up with me.

Jennifer: I'm so sorry. What 2. __________?

Stan: She didn't say. Maybe she was 3. __________ with me. Am I a boring person?

Jennifer: No. You're very interesting. That's why I'm your friend.

Stan: I'm pretty 4. __________ about this. I didn't expect it at all.

Jennifer: She didn't express anything?

Stan: No. This is so confusing!

Jennifer: Keep your head up. You can find someone 5. __________.

Stan: I'm not so sure. How about you? How are you doing?

Jennifer: Well . . . I have some news, but I can tell you later.

Stan: I thought we were friends.

Jennifer: Michael asked me to 6. __________ him. I said *yes*.

Stan: Wow. Congratulations!

Jennifer: Are you sure you're OK?

Stan: Of course. I'm really happy for you.

Jennifer: Thanks, Stan. Let's go have a drink. You shouldn't be alone tonight.

A. Synonyms

Match the word in bold with its synonym.

down	dull
boring	surprised
shocked	say
express	unhappy
alone	by yourself

B. Fill in the Blanks

*Use the words in bold from **A** to complete the sentences.*

1. It's difficult for me to ____________ my feelings because I'm shy.
2. Uncle Lynn doesn't have a computer. It's so ____________ when I go to his house.
3. When she's ____________ at night, she feels afraid.
4. Sad songs always get me ____________.
5. Emma was ____________ by the news. She didn't believe it.

C. Meanings in Context

Choose the meaning of the sentence in the conversation.

1. You shouldn't feel embarrassed about anything.
- **a.** You can share everything with me.
- **b.** You should hide your feelings.

2. Ashley broke up with me.
- **a.** Ashley broke some of my things.
- **b.** Ashley left me.

3. I'm so sorry.
- **a.** I made a mistake.
- **b.** I feel bad for you.

4. I didn't expect it at all.
- **a.** It was a big shock to me.
- **b.** I had a feeling about it.

5. Keep your head up.
- **a.** Try to think about good things.
- **b.** Don't look at the ground.

6. You shouldn't be alone tonight.
- **a.** You need more space.
- **b.** You need to be with a friend.

D. Language Tips

Asking about Someone's Feelings

In Negative Situations	In All Situations
Is everything OK / alright?	What happened?
What's wrong?	Why are you so (*emotion adjective*)?
Why the long face?	

Grammar

Participial Adjectives

Usage

Present Participial Adjectives(-ing)	Past Participial Adjectives(-ed)
Present participials(-ing) are used to describe the causes of feelings. The book is boring.	Past participials(-ed) are used to describe feelings. I feel bored when I read the book.

Paired Adjectives

Verb	-ing Adjective	-ed Adjective
bore	boring	bored
embarrass	embarrassing	embarrassed
interest	interesting	interested
shock	shocking	shocked
confuse	confusing	confused
tire	tiring	tired
excite	exciting	excited
satisfy	satisfying	satisfied
frighten	frightening	frightened
worry	worrying	worried

The basketball game **excited** me.
I was **excited** by the basketball game.
I had fun at the basketball game because it was **exciting**.

Usage Note

Verb + -ing words and **-ing adjectives** look the same. Pay attention to how they are used.

For Example:
The dog is **frightening** the boy.
(the present continuous)
The dog is **frightening**.
(-ing adjective)

Past Participial Adjectives with Prepositions

Some past participials(-ed) are followed by a preposition and a noun.

be bored with	be tired of
be embarrassed about	be excited about
be interested in	be satisfied with
be shocked about / by	be frightened of
be confused by	be worried about

I'm tired of the weather. It always rains in Seattle.
She's not **worried about** the test. She always does well in French.

A. Choose the Feeling

Write the best adjective given to describe each situation.

embarrassing	confusing	exciting	frightening	shocking	tiring	satisfying	worrying

1. We had a good meal in an Italian restaurant. ______________
2. There are too many road signs. ______________
3. I ran in the park for two hours. ______________
4. I wore two different shoes to school today. ______________
5. Jay lost a lot of money. His financial situation isn't good. ______________
6. I never watch horror movies because they scare me. ______________
7. I can't believe it! Mr. Lee is leaving his wife for another woman! ______________
8. My heart beats fast when I jump out of an airplane. I love the feeling! ______________

B. Words in Context

Choose the answer.

1. Helen Keller **inspired** many people. Her story is inspired / inspiring.
2. Let's go to the beach and **relax**. Taking a rest at the beach is relaxed / relaxing.
3. I didn't want to **embarrass** you. Unfortunately, you look embarrassing / embarrassed.
4. This TV show **bores** me. The story is bored / boring.
5. Mr. Starr likes to **encourage** people. His students seem encouraged / encouraging to study more.
6. Modern art **interests** Vicky. She's interested / interesting in the topic.
7. Your dad **frightens** me. He's really frightened / frightening.
8. The news **pleases** me. I'm pleased / pleasing.

C. Correct the Mistakes

Fix the errors in the passage.

excited

Most of us are ~~excite~~ by Leonardo DiCaprio's films. Movies such as *Titanic* and *The Beach* are popular and interested. But he isn't satisfy with just acting. Leonardo is shocking by the damage to the environment, so he works hard to save the earth. He's also worried in wild animals. In 2010, he gave $1,000,000 to Russia to save its tigers. The Russian leader, Vladimir Putin, called him a "real man." But Leonardo embarrassing about this. We never get tiring of Leonardo DiCaprio's films. We're interested with his kind acts as well.

Reading

Before You Read

Look at the pictures. Do you think animals have feelings? Do they also have intelligence?

Do Animals Have Feelings?

Track 34

While You Read

1. What was René Descartes' opinion about animals and emotions?

2. Which animals are playful?

3. How are monkeys like humans?

To the famous philosopher René Descartes, only humans had emotions. Animals were just machines — they didn't have the ability to think. Today, there is a lot of evidence about animals' feelings.

Animals can feel more than basic emotions like the fear observed when they run away from danger. According to scientists, the moods of animals such as elephants, geese, and bears show a sharp change after a loved one dies. Penguins are the same way. In fact, two adult penguins at the London Zoo once stopped eating when their baby was stolen. Animals' emotions are more complex than previously thought. Dolphins and rats are as playful and cheerful as children. They are fun-loving animals. Baboons, a type of monkey, feel stress just like a human.

Some scientists still believe that animals have no feelings. They say that animals only act in certain ways to get a prize, such as food. Animals don't talk, so we can't be sure about their thoughts. What do you think? Do animals have emotions? If so, should humans treat them in a different way?

A. Word Definitions

Use the clues to fill in the blanks with the word choices given. Change the word form if necessary.

philosopher	human	emotion	ability	evidence	according to	fear	mood

1. There is a lot of ____________ that smoking is bad. (shows something is true)
2. Many scientists study these caves. ____________ lived here a long time ago. (person)
3. ____________ the weatherman on TV, a storm is coming. (as told by someone)
4. Love is a powerful ____________, and it can make people do unusual things. (feeling)
5. The famous English ____________ John Locke was born in 1632. (thinker)
6. Many people in Europe have the ____________ to speak several languages. (level of skill)
7. Kathy has a strong ____________ of spiders and snakes. (feeling of being afraid)
8. Terry is always in a bad ____________ on Monday mornings. (state of mind)

B. Words with Different Meanings

Match the word in bold with its definition.

1 The news stories about the car company caused a **sharp** drop in sales. ______
I need a new knife because my old one isn't **sharp** enough. ______
Definition: ⓐ *adj.* happens suddenly and strongly ⓑ *adj.* can cut things easily

2 Doing our homework every night is important. Our teacher puts a lot of **stress** on it. ______
Students feel a lot of **stress** when they have to take final exams. ______
Definition: ⓐ *n.* special attention to something ⓑ *n.* pressure

3 Many pet owners **treat** their animals like their own children. ______
Jim's father promised to bring him a **treat** from New York. ______
Definition: ⓐ *v.* to act towards someone or something ⓑ *n.* something special that you enjoy

C. Multiple Choice

Circle the answers.

1. What did René Descartes think about animals?
   a. Animals could think just like humans.
   b. Animals could learn how to use machines.
   c. Animals had the same feelings as humans.
   d. Animals couldn't think like humans.

2. How do animals probably feel when they run away from danger?
   a. They feel angry.
   b. They feel afraid.
   c. They feel hungry.
   d. They feel sad.

3. Why did the two penguins at the London Zoo stop eating?
   a. They didn't like the new food.
   b. Their zookeeper suddenly died.
   c. Someone took their baby away.
   d. They couldn't feel any emotions.

4. What special thing do rats sometimes do?
   a. Show fear
   b. Sing songs
   c. Have fun
   d. Steal things

UNIT 8 All in Good Fun

1. What do you do on weekends?
2. Is your life exciting or boring?
3. How often do you meet up with friends?

Words & Expressions

Listen and write the sentence number of the activity in the box. Track 35

Free-Time Activities

attend a concert

watch a sporting event

visit a museum

go to KTV

go shopping

go to the movies

go on a picnic

go to a party

go to the beach

go for a bike ride

play a musical instrument

play a sport

Practice

Talk to a partner.

- Who joins you at KTV?
- How often do you go for a bike ride?
- What is the best place to go on a picnic?
- Which activities do you like to do with your friends?

Listen Up

Listen and check the information you hear. Track 36

- ☐ I don't like to ride a bike when the path is too crowded.
- ☐ My friends and I go on a picnic every two weeks.
- ☐ I go for a bike ride on weekends.
- ☐ I enjoy staying home and watching TV.
- ☐ Sometimes, I relax by reading in the park.

- ☐ I am a big fan of martial arts.
- ☐ Checking out art museums is a really interesting activity.
- ☐ Jazz is my favorite type of music.
- ☐ I practice playing the guitar in my free time.
- ☐ I don't like to attend concerts.

Act It Out

Practice the conversations with the word choices given.

attend concerts	watch TV	play a musical instrument		going to the movies
rock	jazz	classical	hip-hop	
the news	sitcoms	movies	sports programs	
piano	guitar	violin	flute	trumpet
action film	drama	comedy	horror film	romance

1. A: Do you ______________________?
B: Yes. I like _____________ music the most.

2. A: How often do you _____________?
B: I watch TV for an hour every day. I like to watch _____________.

3. A: Can you ______________________________?
B: Yes. I can play the _____________. / No, but I want to take _____________ lessons.

4. A: Do you enjoy ______________________?
B: Yes, I do. I usually watch a(n) ___________.

Did You Know...?

Put the words in the appropriate columns. Some words can be used with more than one verb.

a meeting　an amusement park　a friend　a basketball game　a city　a club

go to	attend	visit

Conversation

Making Plans

Listen and fill in the blanks with the word choices given. Track 37

opinion	live	romance	relaxing	delicious	fan

Amanda and Greg are talking about their plans for tonight.

Amanda: Hey, Greg. What are you doing tonight?

Greg: Hi, Amanda. I'm not sure. Would you like to go to a movie?

Amanda: Sure. I love movies. What type of movie?

Greg: Let me think . . . Are you a(n) 1. ___________ of action movies?

Amanda: Action movies aren't my cup of tea. What do you think about seeing a(n) 2. ___________ movie?

Greg: They're not my thing. Maybe seeing a movie isn't a good idea. Do you like going to concerts? There's a concert in the park tonight.

Amanda: That's a great idea. I love listening to 3. ___________ music.

Greg: Great. What's your 4. ___________ of classical music? It's a Bach concert.

Amanda: I like Bach's music a lot. Attending a classical concert sounds very 5. ___________.

Greg: Cool. I can pick you up. Do you want to have dinner before the concert? I know a good Indian restaurant.

Amanda: I'm not a big fan of Indian food. What do you think of having Italian food?

Greg: That sounds good to me. Italian food is 6. ___________. See you then.

Amanda: Bye.

A. Word Definitions

Use the clues to fill in the blanks with the word choices given.

type	fan	romance	concert	live	opinion	classical	relaxing

1. I didn't like the movie at all. What is your ____________? (idea)
2. Listening to ____________ music helps me go to sleep at night. (by Mozart or Bach)
3. Jason is a big ____________ of comic books. He has a collection of them. (really likes)
4. My weekend in the countryside was very ____________. (peaceful)
5. Six different bands are playing in the ____________. (show)
6. Jenny loves ____________ music. She goes to clubs every weekend. (not recorded)
7. I don't like that ____________ of food. There is too much oil in it. (kind)
8. This book is a(n) ____________ about a young couple in France. (love)

B. Meanings in Context

Choose the meaning of the sentence in the conversation.

1. I'm not sure.
a. There is no doubt.
b. I don't know.

2. Action movies aren't my cup of tea.
a. I don't really like them.
b. I think they are the best.

3. They are not my thing.
a. I lost one of them.
b. I'm not interested in them.

4. I can pick you up.
a. I'm stronger than you are.
b. I'm able to give you a ride.

5. I'm not a big fan of Indian food.
a. Indian food isn't my favorite type of food.
b. Indian food tastes very good.

6. That sounds good to me.
a. That's a great idea.
b. That's beautiful music.

C. Language Tips

Talking about Likes and Dislikes

Question	Response	
	Likes	***Dislikes***
Do you like . . .?	I like . . . (very much / a lot).	I don't like . . .
Do you enjoy . . .?	I enjoy . . .	I hate . . .
Are you a fan of . . .?	I'm a big fan of . . .	I'm not a fan of . . .
	I'm a big . . . fan.	. . . is not for me.
	I'm crazy about . . .	. . . is not my cup of tea.
		. . . is not my thing.

Practice the sentence patterns with the choices below.

reading novels	traveling	old movies
collecting stamps	the Internet	Chinese food
talking on the phone	the New York Yankees	knitting

Grammar

Gerunds and Infinitives

Usage

Both gerunds (Verb + -ing form) and infinitives (to + base form) can be used as the **subject, complement**, or **object** of a sentence.

subject	Seeing a movie isn't a good idea. To make mistakes is good for language learning.
complement	James' favorite sport is swimming. Kim's dream is to become a dancer.
object	I love listening to live music. Alex wants to drink some fruit juice.

Usage Note

1. Gerunds are most commonly used as the subject or complement of a sentence.
2. Only gerunds are used as the object of a preposition.

For Example:

What do you think of having Italian food?

~~What do you think of to have Italian food?~~

Signal Words

Verbs are often followed by gerunds or infinitives.

gerunds	admit imagine	avoid keep	consider miss	mind regret	enjoy suggest	finish quit
infinitives	agree hope	ask learn	choose plan	decide promise	expect want	fail need
gerunds or infinitives	continue	begin	start	hate	like	love

Chris **enjoys** fishing with his kid.
Bryan **refused** to go to the meeting.
Mike **hates** shopping / to shop.

Different Meanings

Some verbs can be followed by gerunds or infinitives, but there will be a difference in meaning.

Verb	Example	Meaning
remember	I **remembered** sending the e-mail.	I sent the e-mail, and I remembered the action.
	I **remembered** to send the e-mail.	I needed to send the e-mail, and I did it.
stop	The man **stopped** smoking.	He doesn't smoke anymore.
	The man **stopped** to smoke.	He stopped because he wanted to smoke.
go on	Kate **went on** working as a nurse.	She kept working as a nurse.
	Kate **went on** to work as a nurse.	Her next step was to become a nurse.

A. Fill in the Blanks

Use the gerund or infinitive form of the words given to complete the sentences.

live	speak	take	travel	go	exercise	help	make

1. Dan promised ________________ his son to an amusement park.
2. Felix wants ________________ all over the world.
3. I avoid ________________ for more than two hours in the gym.
4. Isaac keeps ________________ noise while I'm working.
5. I chose ________________ in the city because it's exciting.
6. How did you learn ________________ English so well?
7. Tyler always asks ________________ to the bathroom during class.
8. Eva agreed ________________ me with my school project.

B. Complete the Dialogue

Use the words given to complete the dialogue.

enjoy	hope	need	love	miss	suggest	mind	plan

Sandy: I am taking a semester off. I **1.** ______________ to make money.
Cam: What are you doing?
Sandy: I'm working at the post office. I deliver letters.
Cam: Do you **2.** ______________ delivering mails instead of going to school?
Sandy: No. I **3.** ______________ working at the post office. I also **4.** ______________ to walk around the neighborhood.
Cam: I **5.** ______________ to see you back at school soon, Sandy.
Sandy: Me too. I **6.** ______________ seeing my classmates. I **7.** ______________ to return next year.
Cam: Well, I **8.** ______________ working hard.
Sandy: Don't worry, Cam. I am a hard worker.

C. Correct the Mistakes

Fix the errors in the passage.

What do you regret the most in your life? A newspaper asked people the question. Many people remembered ~~to quit~~ quitting a good job. Some people admitted to leave school too early. Others missed to seeing an old boyfriend or girlfriend. Many fathers regret not spend enough time with their children. They avoided to get along with them because they were busy. They didn't stop talking to their kids. What about you? Start think about what is important in your life and decide making changes.

Reading

Before You Read

Look at the pictures. What are the people doing? What activities do you want to do for exciting?

Make Your Life More Extreme

Track 38

Most people agree that ironing is boring. However, would you like to try extreme ironing? Extreme ironing is a little different from normal ironing. Instead of in your home, you do it on a boat, skateboard, or mountain. This is an extreme sport.

An extreme sport is a fun and risky activity. It's also a little dangerous. Take shark cage diving, for example. Divers go into the ocean with great white sharks. The divers stay in a cage. This way, they don't become the shark's lunch.

Everyone knows about the Running of the Bulls. This is an annual event in Pamplona, Spain. Bulls chase participants through the city streets. Injuries are common because the bulls are big, strong, and angry.

Would you like to ride your bike on the Road of Death? This is a road in Bolivia. Locals gave it that name because it is the most dangerous road in the world. It is high up and very narrow. However, some bikers like it because of the adventure and beautiful view.

Do you feel bored with life? Maybe an extreme sport is the answer.

While You Read

1. *Which sport takes place in the water?*
2. *Which sport requires people to run?*
3. *Which sport do you think is the most dangerous?*

A. Word Definitions

Use the clues to fill in the blanks with the word choices given. Change the word form if necessary.

agree	extreme	dive	annual	participant	chase	local

1. Bungee jumping is a(n) __________ sport in which people jump from a high place. (very unusual and dangerous)
2. I __________ that knowledge of Chinese is helpful to learn Japanese. (have the same opinion)
3. Some visitors throw trash on the ground. The __________ are angry about this. (people who live in the place)
4. The man __________ into the river from a height of 20 meters. (jump into deep water)
5. I always have fun at our __________ company trip. (yearly)
6. Some scientists __________ storms to learn about storms. (go after)
7. __________ in the survey get gifts from the company. (someone who takes part in an activity)

B. Complete the Passage

Use the correct form of the words given to complete the passage.

risky	injuries	dangerous	adventure

Are you missing something in your life? Do you have extra energy to get rid of? If you said *yes* to these questions, an extreme sport like volcano boarding is perfect for you. Visitors to Nicaragua's Cerro Negro volcano can slide down the mountain at speeds of up to 80 kilometers per hour. Going down an active volcano can be **1.** __________. Some parts of Cerro Negro are **2.** __________, but the boarding area isn't. **3.** __________ can sometimes happen, but it's as safe as snowboarding. Are you ready for a one-of-a-kind **4.** __________?

C. Multiple Choice

Circle the answers.

1. Where could extreme ironing be done?
   a. On your balcony
   b. In a convenience store
   c. On a skateboard
   d. In your living room

2. What does the article say about shark cage diving?
   a. People oppose shark cage diving.
   b. Participants dive with great whites.
   c. It is a boring activity these days.
   d. Divers eat lunch in the cage.

3. What is true about the Running of the Bulls?
   a. Injuries happen all the time there.
   b. The bulls run away from participants.
   c. It happens once a month in Pamplona.
   d. The bulls usually stay in a cage.

4. Why do bikers go to the Road of Death?
   a. Their relatives died on the road.
   b. There are bulls on the road.
   c. They enjoy the pretty scenery.
   d. It is in a historic valley.

UNIT 9

Game Time

1. What do you do for exercise?
2. Who are your favorite sports stars?
3. Do you like to exercise alone or with friends?

Words & Expressions

Listen and write the sentence number of the sport in the box. Track 39

Types of Sports

play baseball

go golfing

play football

play volleyball

play hockey

go bowling

go jogging

lift weights

play badminton

do tae kwon do

play basketball

play soccer

Write the name of the sport in the appropriate columns.

Individual Sport	Team Sport

Practice

Talk to a partner.

- Which of these sports do you play?
- Which sports do you like to watch on TV?
- Which sports do you think are boring?
- Do you think sports are important?

Listen Up

Task I *Listen and complete the chart.* Track 40

Korean	Russian	Brazilian
Moscow	São Paulo	Seoul
golf	hockey	soccer

	Nationality	City	Favorite Sport	Play / Watch
Fabio				
Shin-soo				
Elena				

Task II *Listen again and check* ***True*** *or* ***False.***

	True	False
1. Fabio is a rich man from Brazil.	☐	☐
2. Golf is the most popular sport in South Korea.	☐	☐
3. Golf is an expensive sport to play in South Korea.	☐	☐
4. Elena is too busy to play a sport.	☐	☐
5. Elena broke her nose twice this year.	☐	☐

Act It Out

Practice the conversations with the word choices given.

football	baseball	basketball	volleyball	hockey
lift weights	do tae kwon do	swim	go mountain climbing	
golfing	bowling	jogging	surfing	
this afternoon	on Saturday	next weekend		

1. A: I often play ______________ with my friends.
B: Really? I prefer to ______________.

2. A: I want to watch a ______________ game on TV.
B: You're so lazy. Don't just watch. Go out and play ______________.

3. A: I want to go ______________, but my friends are busy.
B: I can go with you. We can do it ______________.

Did You Know...?

Match the sport with the place. Some sports are played in the same place.

a. park	**b.** field
c. pool	**d.** gym
e. course	**f.** court

_______ **1.** lift weights _______ **2.** go swimming
_______ **3.** go jogging _______ **4.** play soccer
_______ **5.** play basketball _______ **6.** go golfing
_______ **7.** play football _______ **8.** play volleyball

Conversation

Sports Talk

Listen and fill in the blanks with the word choices given. Track 41

knee	asleep	hard	leading	meet up	a lot

Jerry calls his friend Adam on the phone.

Jerry: Hi, Adam. What's up?

Adam: Hey, Jerry. I was watching a basketball game, but I fell **1.** ___________. It's almost over.

Jerry: Orlando is playing Miami, right? Who's winning?

Adam: Orlando is **2.** ___________ by eight. Miami is pretty weak.

Jerry: Great! I hate Miami. Did you see Saturday's game?

Adam: No. I was busy. I was working out at the gym.

Jerry: You work out **3.** ___________. Are you still playing basketball?

Adam: A little bit, but my back hurts right now. I hurt it while I was playing basketball with friends on Sunday.

Jerry: That's too bad, man.

Adam: I need to recover and get back in shape.

Jerry: While you were playing basketball, I was watching TV. I have **4.** ___________ problems, so I don't exercise enough.

Adam: When I'm healthy, I play a lot. I want to join the school team.

Jerry: Then you should practice **5.** ___________. Basketball requires a lot of skill.

Adam: And you have to be tall.

Jerry: I know. I guess basketball isn't for me. Let's **6.** ___________ and watch a DVD.

Adam: Sounds good.

A. Words with Different Meanings

Match the word in bold with its definition.

1 The Rangers are **leading** the game. ______
Our tour guide **led** us all over Shanghai. ______
Definition: ⓐ *v.* to take someone somewhere ⓑ *v.* to be winning a game

2 Jamal and his brother play computer games all day. Their muscles are very **weak**. ______
I speak English well, but my writing is **weak**. ______
Definition: ⓐ *adj.* not good ⓑ *adj.* not strong

3 My back **hurts** when I stand up. ______
He **hurt** his knee in the soccer game. ______
Definition: ⓐ *v.* to feel pain ⓑ *v.* to damage something

4 Helen worked **hard** to improve her test scores. ______
This year's exam was very **hard**. Many students failed. ______
Definition: ⓐ *adj.* difficult ⓑ *adv.* with a lot of effort

B. Meanings in Context

Choose the meaning of the sentence in the conversation.

1. It's almost over.
a. It's almost on the top.
b. It's close to the end.

2. I was working out at the gym.
a. I had a job at the gym.
b. I was exercising at the gym.

3. I need to recover and get back in shape.
a. I should get healthy again.
b. I need to cover up my body.

4. Basketball requires a lot of skill.
a. Skill is important for basketball.
b. Basketball teaches you many things.

5. I guess basketball isn't for me.
a. This isn't my basketball.
b. Basketball is not the right sport for me.

C. Language Tips

Talking about Injuries

Body Part	Incident			Explanation
My (*body part*) hurts.	I	hurt broke injured	my (*body part*).	I have (*body part*) problems. I have a(n) (*body part*) problem. I have (*body part*) pain. I have a bad (*body part*). I have a(n) (*body part*) injury.

Rewrite the sentences using the sentence patterns above. Use different patterns for each blank.

1. My back hurts. ▸ ______________________________
2. Sam broke his ankle. ▸ ______________________________
3. I injured my elbow. ▸ ______________________________
4. My mother hurt her knee. ▸ ______________________________

Grammar

Past Continuous Tense

Use the **past continuous tense** to describe longer actions in the past.

Statements

Subject	Past Tense of Be Verb	(Not)	Verb + –ing
I	was	(not)	reading a novel.
You	were	(not)	exercising.
He / She / It	was	(not)	looking at me.
We / You / They	were	(not)	traveling through China.

Questions

Question	Response
Were you studying at university in 2014?	Yes, I was. / No, I wasn't.
Was Nick working last weekend?	Yes, he was. / No, he wasn't.
What were the two boys doing yesterday?	They were studying for a test.
Who was singing in the room?	My younger sister was (singing).

Usage

A short action during a longer action in the past

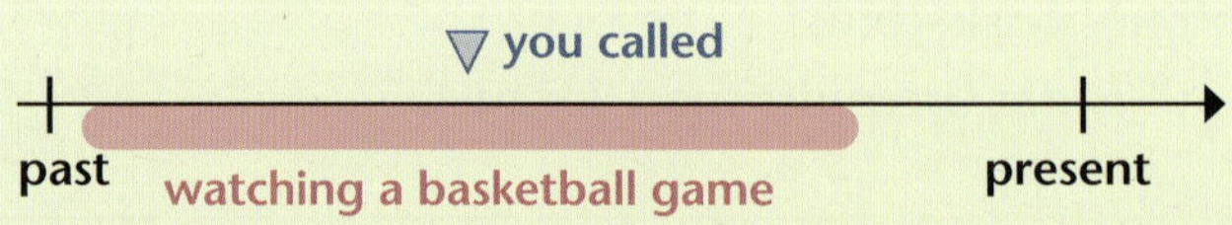

I was watching a basketball game when you called.

A longer action at a certain time

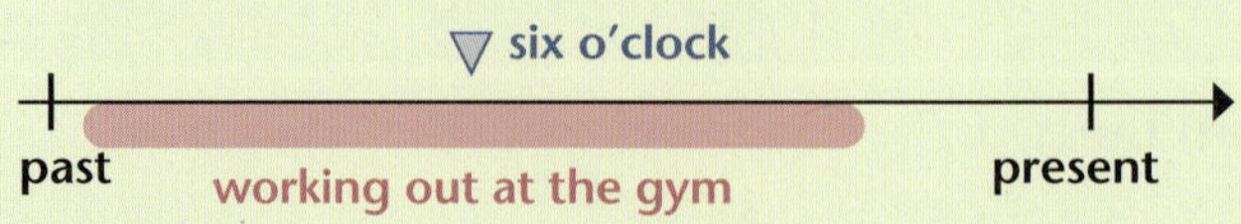

At six o'clock, I was working out at the gym.

Two longer actions at the same time in the past

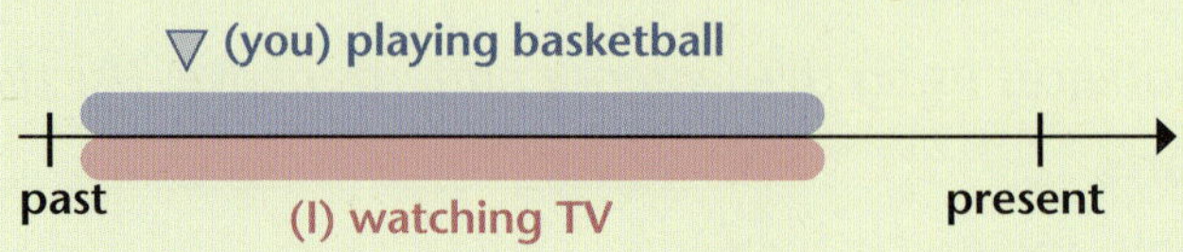

While you were playing basketball, I was watching TV.

A. Match

Match the question with the response.

	Question		Response
______	1. Who were you talking to at the park yesterday?		a. He was at the London office.
______	2. Were you playing volleyball on Saturday morning?		b. I was talking to my uncle.
______	3. Why was Alice yelling at Derek this afternoon?		c. Yes. We met at two p.m. in the gym.
______	4. Was the basketball team practicing last Tuesday?		d. I was having lunch with Eva.
______	5. What were you doing at noon on Monday?		e. Alex. He was writing an e-mail.
______	6. Where was Chris working last month?		f. No. I was watching a movie at home.
______	7. Who was using the computer earlier?		g. Yes. They were making fun of his ears.
______	8. Were they making jokes about the boy?		h. He broke her phone.

B. Fill in the Blanks

Change the verb into the past continuous form to complete the sentence.

1. I ________________ (listen) to music when the phone rang.
2. My parents ________________ (sleep) at the time of the earthquake.
3. Henry ________________ (study) in the library last Sunday.
4. The man fell asleep while he ________________ (ride) on the train.
5. At three p.m., I ________________ (sing) with my friends at KTV.
6. My brothers ________________ (jog) yesterday morning.
7. Vicki ________________ (work) all day yesterday.
8. While Ken ________________ (talk) to Jenny, someone stole his bags.
9. It started to rain while we ________________ (hike) in the mountains.

C. Correct the Mistakes

Fix the errors in the story.

happened

I was riding my motorcycle when something bad ~~happening~~. A car in front of me stopped quickly. My motorcycle hit the back of the car, and I flew into the air. While I fly through the air, I think about my family. I don't remember much after that. When I woke up, a doctor talked to me. The doctor asked me, "Was you drinking last night?" "I wasn't drinking before I get on my motorcycle," I said. "I read at home when my friend invited me to his house." While I was speak, the doctor checked my eyes. He told me to be more careful on my motorcycle. While I rode home in my wife's car, I feel thankful for my good luck.

Reading

Before You Read

Look at the pictures. Is there anything unusual about the surfer? What do you think the reading is about?

Sports Hero

Track 42

While You Read

1. What happened to Bethany?

2. What is the name of her book?

Do you surf? Bethany Hamilton surfs a lot. Her parents taught her how, and she was in her first competition when she was eight. Even before she was ten, she wanted to be a professional. She entered more competitions and got a company, Rip Curl, to support her.

Then, one day in 2003, a shark attacked her. She lost her left arm and over 60 percent of her blood. She nearly lost her life. Most people are scared of the water after a shark attack. Not Bethany! Just one month later she was back in the water practicing. She kept working towards her goal, kept competing, and turned professional in 2007.

In 2009, she took second place in the Billabong ASP World Junior Championship in Australia. She wrote a book called *Soul Surfer* and was on *The Oprah Winfrey Show*. There is even a movie about her story with Dennis Quaid and Helen Hunt. Bethany is one of the world's top surfers and an inspiration to us all. To find out more about her, go to www.bethanyhamilton.com.

Facts about Bethany Hamilton

Full Name: Bethany Meilani Hamilton
Hometown: Hanalei, Kauai, Hawaii
Born: February eighth, 1990
Height: 187 cm
Weight: 64 kg
Pet: One dog — Hanalei
Motto: "Love life!"

A. Words with Different Meanings

Match the word in bold with its definition.

1. You can now **surf** the Internet on your cell phone. ______
   I love to **surf** in Hawaii. The weather there is fantastic! ______
   Definition: ⓐ *v.* to ride on waves ⓑ *v.* to look through information online

2. As a health **professional**, he works with sick people all day. ______
   The young skating star became **professional** at age 15. ______
   Definition: ⓐ *n.* a worker with special training ⓑ *adj.* doing something for pay

3. I'm old enough to **support** myself now. ______
   I hurt my leg, so I'm wearing an ankle **support**. ______
   Definition: ⓐ *v.* to give money, food, or housing ⓑ *n.* something to hold a weak part of the body

B. Synonyms

Match the word in bold with its synonym.

competition •	• role model
nearly •	• afraid
scared •	• almost
goal •	• contest
inspiration •	• aim

C. Fill in the Blanks

*Use the words in bold from **B** to complete the sentence.*

1. Henry is a great dancer. He won the dancing ____________ last week.
2. Linda doesn't have any pets. She's ____________ of animals.
3. He always helps poor people. He's a(n) ____________ to me.
4. The government's ____________ is to give jobs for everybody again.
5. Be careful on the road. I was ____________ killed last time.

D. Multiple Choice

Circle the answers.

1. When did Bethany start surfing in competitions?
   a. She started when she was 60 years old.
   b. Bethany was eight when she started.
   c. Her first competition was in 1990.
   d. Bethany first competed in 2003.

2. What happened when a shark attacked Bethany?
   a. She was killed.
   b. She became less famous.
   c. She started surfing.
   d. The shark bit off her left arm.

3. Which statement is NOT true?
   a. Bethany wrote a book.
   b. Her story was made into a movie.
   c. She was scared of the water.
   d. She appeared on *The Oprah Winfrey Show*.

4. What is true about Bethany's website?
   a. You can learn about Bethany on it.
   b. It shows you how to surf better.
   c. It's the best place to study sharks.
   d. You can help her win championships.

UNIT 10

Rain or Shine

1. What kind of weather do you like best?
2. How weather affects your mood?
3. Do you watch the weather report on the news?

Words & Expressions

Fill in the blanks with the word choices given.

Nouns	lightning	showers	clouds	Adjectives	foggy	humid	sunny
Verbs	snowing	blowing	raining				

Weather Conditions

It's ________.

It's ________.

There are no ________.

The wind is ________ strongly.

It's very hot and ________ today.

There was thunder after the ________.

It's really cloudy. There could be ________.

It's so ________.

It's warm and ________.

Listen and write the sentence number in the box. Track 43

Practice

Talk to a partner.

- Do you know any tips on how to prepare for a typhoon?
- Have you seen snowstorm?
- Do you like to go skiing or ice-skating?

Listen Up

Task I *Listen and write the places of the city(Prague, Taipei, or Bangkok).* Track 44

Task II *Listen again and fill in the blanks with the word choices given.*

snowy heat wave wet humid storm warm clothes sun foggy

1. Today is a cold and ______________ day in Prague. It is important to wear ______________.
2. There is a ______________ in Taipei. It is ______________. Try to be careful. It's also ______________ and difficult to see.
3. Bangkok is going through a ______________. It's very hot and ______________. You shouldn't stay in the ______________ for too long.

Act It Out

Practice the conversations with the word choices given.

spring	summer	fall	winter		
warm	hot	cool	cold		
sky	sun	wind	fog	rain	
clear	sunny	windy	foggy	rainy	
sunglasses	a swimsuit	a scarf	a jacket	a raincoat	an umbrella

1. **A:** My favorite season is ______________.
   B: Me too. I also like ______________ weather.
2. **A:** Look at the ______________.
   B: Yeah. It's a ______________ day.
3. **A:** Did you hear the weather report? It's going to be ______________ today.
   B: We need to bring ______________.

Did You Know...?

Noun	Verb	Adjective	Noun	Verb	Adjective
rain	rain	rainy	cloud		cloudy
sun	shine	sunny	fog		foggy
wind	blow	windy	storm		stormy

There is a lot of **snow** today. It's **snowing** today. Today is a **snowy** day.

Conversation

A Weekend at the Lake

Listen and fill in the blanks with the word choices given. Track 45

swimsuit	sunny	lightning	fun	check	enough

Sandra and Stacey are talking in the university cafeteria.

Sandra: Hey, Stacey. Do you have plans for the weekend?

Stacey: I want to go to the lake.

Sandra: Sounds like 1. ___________. Can I join you?

Stacey: Sure. Will you come with John?

Sandra: I'm going to ask him. He looks good in a 2. ___________.

Stacey: That's cool, but the weather won't be good 3. ___________ to swim on Saturday.

Sandra: Did you 4. ___________ the weather report?

Stacey: Of course. It's going to be windy on Saturday. The temperature will be about 20 degrees. It will also be foggy.

Sandra: That's too bad. That's too cold for swimming. How about flying kites?

Stacey: Good idea. The weather will be perfect for that.

Sandra: Really? I hope we don't have 5. ___________. It can be dangerous. Is Jason going to come too?

Stacey: Yes, he is. The four of us are going to have a picnic.

Sandra: Wonderful. What are we going to do on Sunday?

Stacey: Sunday will be warm, clear, and 6. ___________. That's great weather for swimming.

Sandra: We can go fishing too. Maybe we will have fish for dinner.

Stacey: I can't wait.

A. Fill in the Blanks

Use the words given to complete the sentences.

warm	lightning	sunny	windy	fog	clear

1. Saturday will be ______________. The weather will be perfect for flying kites.
2. There will be ______________ on Saturday. It will be difficult to see the sky.
3. Sandra is worried. It is dangerous to fly kites when there is ______________.
4. On Sunday, it's going to be ______________. They will be able to see well.
5. Stacey thinks ______________ weather is best for swimming.
6. They won't be cold on Sunday. The temperature is going to be ______________.

B. Word Definitions

Use the clues to fill in the blanks.

1. We're going to the beach this afternoon. Don't forget your **s**____________. (wear this in water)
2. The TV station gives weather **r**____________ every hour. (information)
3. Water starts to boil at a **t**____________ of 100 degrees Celsius. (how hot or cold)
4. It's **d**____________ to swim in the lake. The water is too deep. (not safe)
5. We had a **w**____________ time when we went sailing on the bay. (excellent)

C. Meanings in Context

Choose the meaning of the sentence in the conversation.

1. That's cool. **a.** I like it. **b.** It's not hot.	**2.** The temperature will be about 20°C. **a.** It'll be warmer or colder than 20°C. **b.** It'll only be colder than 20°C.
3. Good idea. **a.** You are kind. **b.** That sounds good.	**3.** I can't wait. **a.** I'm excited about this. **b.** I have to go now.

D. Language Tips

Asking about Weather

Did you check the weather report?	Will it be (*weather adjective*) tomorrow?
How will the weather be?	What will the weather be like?
What will the temperature be next week?	

Describing Weather Conditions

Good	Bad
The weather will be great.	It'll be windy.
It'll be clear and sunny.	The weather will be cloudy.
It'll be sunny out / outside.	It'll be a rainy day.

Grammar

Simple Future Tense

Statements

Subject + be + (not) + going to + base form of verb + (*time*).
It's (not) going to be windy on Saturday. Jason is (not) going to come.

Subject + will + (not) + base form of verb + (*time*).
The weather will (not) be good enough to go swimming. David will (not) go to work next Monday.

Usage Note

We often use contractions of **be** and **will** with pronouns in speaking (it's, it'll, we're, we'll, etc.). We also use contractions for **will not** (won't).

Questions

Question	Response
Is Sunday going to be warm? When are they going to arrive?	Yes, it is. / No, it isn't. They're going to arrive at 3:00.
Will you come with John? What will the temperature be on Saturday?	Yes, I will. / No, I won't. It will be about 20 degrees.

Be Going to vs. Will

Usage	Example
be going to or **will** (make predictions)	It's not going to rain tomorrow. It'll be warm and humid. The earth will get warmer in the next ten years.
be going to (talk about plans)	Sylvia is going to meet her friend tomorrow. They're going to build a new house this summer.

Usage Note

We can also use **the present continuous tense** to talk about the future.

For Example:

Mike **is going to visit** his grandparents tomorrow morning.
(Mike **is visiting** his grandparents tomorrow morning.)

Future Time Expressions

today tonight this summer	tomorrow tomorrow morning next week	in January in two weeks on Friday afternoon

A. Match

It's August 20th, and Hans is looking at his calendar. Match the question with the response.

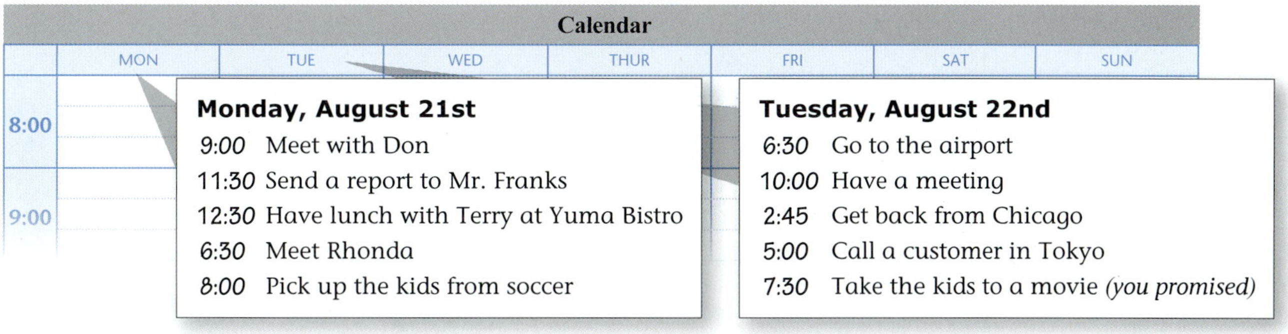

_____ **1.** Who is he going to meet for lunch tomorrow?
_____ **2.** Where will he go early Tuesday morning?
_____ **3.** What will he do on Tuesday night?
_____ **4.** When will he send Mr. Franks a report?
_____ **5.** What is he going to do last on Monday?
_____ **6.** Who is he going to call at five o'clock?

a. He's going to go to Chicago.
b. He'll do that on Monday.
c. He's going to eat with Terry.
d. He's going to see a cartoon.
e. He'll phone someone overseas then.
f. He'll go to get his kids at eight o'clock.

B. Correct the Mistakes

Fix the errors in the passage.

The weather for tomorrow ^is going to be cloudy. There will is some rain in the evening. You will to need an umbrella. It's also going be cold and windy, so you will having to wear warm clothes. The temperature will 13 degrees Celsius. On the weekend, it going to be sunny. The weather will be going good for getting out or playing sports. That's great news for most of us. Winter are going to come soon. Enjoy the nice weather. It's not going to lasting much longer.

C. True or False

*Listen and check **True** or **False**.* Track 46

	True	False
1. Matt is going to make an action movie next.	☐	☐
2. Matt is not going to make a movie in the next year.	☐	☐
3. Matt will go back to Australia.	☐	☐
4. Matt is going to relax.	☐	☐
5. Matt will buy a beautiful home in Australia.	☐	☐
6. Matt is going to stay in Australia for several years.	☐	☐
7. Matt is going to make a film about George Washington.	☐	☐
8. Matt will go to work for a radio station.	☐	☐

Reading

Before You Read

Look at the pictures. Which place looks the nicest? What do you think the reading is about?

Safe at Home

Track 47

While You Read

1. Why are some houses built differently than others?

2. In what way are Taipei 101's neighbors lucky?

Houses protect people from dangers. They have roofs and walls to keep out bad weather like cold wind or heavy rain. Some houses are built with special protection against natural disasters like typhoons or earthquakes.

Igloos are built by the Inuit people of Canada and Greenland. They are made from snow but are actually quite warm inside because the snow holds air. When the air outside is minus 45 degrees Celsius, the air inside can be a more pleasant 16 degrees Celsius.

Stilt houses offer another kind of protection. These houses are built on long sticks over land or water. They stop flood damage when rivers or lakes rise. They also help to keep rats and other animals out. Stilt houses are still found in Vietnam, Cambodia, and in places in South America.

Taipei 101 is a landmark supertall skyscraper in Taipei, Taiwan. Normally, such a tall building would shake and fall down if typhoons or earthquakes occur. It can withstand natural disasters because it has a tuned mass damper, a huge metal ball. The ball hangs from the 92nd to the 88th floor. When Taipei 101 moves, the ball swings and stops the building from shaking into pieces. Lucky for the neighbors!

A. Fill in the Blanks

Use the words given to complete the sentences. Change the word form if necessary.

stick	flood	damage	rise

1. Sales ___________ every year around Christmas.
2. The driver is fine, but there is a lot of ___________ to the car.
3. After two days of heavy rain, the town was ___________.
4. You can make a fire by rubbing ___________ together, but it takes a long time.
5. The ___________ killed a lot of people in the village.
6. Don't ___________ your finger in your nose! It's very rude.
7. There was a ___________ in food prices last year.
8. Listening to loud music can ___________ your ears.

B. Word Definitions

Use the clues to fill in the blanks with the word choices given.

actually	minus	pleasant	protective	earthquake	metal	hang	swing

1. A(n) ___________ in China in the 1500s killed nearly one million people. (shaking of the earth)
2. A lot of children would like to ___________ from tree to tree like a monkey. (move from one side to another)
3. Ray looks pretty young, but he's ___________ 40 years old. (in fact)
4. Don't go outside! It's ___________ 20 degrees out there. (below zero)
5. Some people keep their phones in ___________ cases because they don't want them to break. (safe)
6. The roof is made of ___________. It's really loud when it rains. (a hard, shiny material)
7. The Striebers have a very ___________ house in the woods. I went there with them last winter. (comfortable)
8. Beautiful pictures ___________ in the hall. (be suspended)

C. Classification

Write the type of house next to the matching statement.

ⓐ igloos

ⓑ stilt houses

ⓒ tall buildings

1. These houses which are built over the ground keep people safe from rats and other animals. _____
2. Special homes like these have a roof made from ice. _____
3. These houses have special protection for not shaking against typhoons or earthquakes. _____
4. You can see these houses in Cambodia. _____
5. The walls of these houses are cold, but they still have warm air inside. _____
6. These can have more than 100 floors. _____
7. If you live in a very cold place, this is a good house for you. _____
8. These houses are built on sticks over water or land. _____

UNIT 11

Eating Out

1. What's the best restaurant in your hometown?
2. How many times do you eat out each week?
3. Where would you take someone on a first date?

Words & Expressions

Menu Sections

Task I *Listen and write the sentence number in the box.* Track 48

Harris Ranch Diner

☐	Starters	French fries, potato skins, Buffalo wings
☐	Soups	vegetable, French onion, soup of the day
☐	Salads	Caesar, garden, broccoli
☐	Main dishes	burger, spaghetti, steak, turkey
☐	Desserts	chocolate cake, tiramisu, ice cream
☐	Drinks	soda, fresh fruit juice, beer

Business hours: 11 a.m. to 11:30 p.m. every day
313 Pacific Lane, Stockton, CO 72843
(652) 717-3005

Task II *Complete the sentences with the menu sections from above. Change the word form if necessary.*

1. We eat a ____________ at the beginning of a meal.
2. ____________ are usually sweet. The waiter serves them after a meal.
3. You can find different vegetables in ____________.
4. Green tea is one of Darren's favorite ____________.
5. ____________ are the biggest part of a meal. They'll fill your stomach.
6. We use a spoon, not a fork, to have ____________.

Practice

Talk to a partner.

- What would you order from the menu?
- Which menu options are healthy? Which are not?
- How late does the restaurant stay open on Thursdays?

Listen Up

Task I *Listen and write the dialogue number and the menu section.* Track 49

☐ ____________

☐ ____________

☐ ____________

☐ ____________

☐ ____________

☐ ____________

Task II *Listen and check* ***True*** *or* ***False****.*

	True	False
1. Amelia didn't eat anything today.	☐	☐
2. Natalie is ordering small size.	☐	☐
3. Phil and Pete need more time to decide on their main dishes.	☐	☐
4. Chris has something to drink.	☐	☐
5. The man orders blue cheese dressing.	☐	☐
6. Deborah and Tony both want to eat a lot of food.	☐	☐

Act It Out

Practice the conversations with the word choices given.

starter soup salad main dish
some French fries the soup of the day
the Greek salad the pasta
steak house café buffet sushi bar
steaks sandwiches lobster sashimi
juice soda coffee beer wine

1. A: Do you want a ____________?
B: Sure. I would like ____________, please.

2. A: I know a good ____________ on 19th Avenue.
B: Oh yeah. That restaurant's ____________ is / are great.

3. A: Would you like something to drink?
B: Yes. What types of ____________ do you have?

Did You Know...?

Would you like, could you, *and* ***could / may I*** *are more polite than* ***do you want, can you,*** *and* ***can I.***
Practice saying the following sentences in a more polite way.

1. Can I take your coat?
2. Do you want fries with your meal?
3. Can you hold on for a second?
4. I want two bowls of soup.

Conversation

Dinner Date

Listen and fill in the blanks with the word choices given. Track 50

order	recommend	fine	drink	popular	waitress

Jimmy and Daphne are in a restaurant.

Jimmy: Something smells delicious in here.

Daphne: You're right. I can't wait to order. Oh, our waitress is coming.

Nicole: Hello. Welcome to Barney's Burgers. I'm Nicole, your **1.** __________ for the evening. May I get you something to start?

Daphne: We'll start with the French fries. It's our first time at this restaurant. Could you **2.** __________ any main dishes?

Nicole: Everything is good here, but I really like the chicken sandwich. Or you could try our bacon cheeseburger and mushroom burger. Both are very **3.** __________.

Daphne: OK. I would like the bacon cheeseburger. Hold the tomatoes, please.

Nicole: Sure. One bacon cheeseburger. Hold the tomatoes. How about you, sir?

Jimmy: I'll have the chicken sandwich. Could you give me extra barbecue sauce on the side?

Nicole: Of course. I can add some to your **4.** __________.

Jimmy: Sounds good. Thank you.

Nicole: Do you want anything to **5.** __________?

Jimmy: No, thank you. Water is **6.** __________.

Daphne: I'll have a cup of coffee. Can I have it right away?

Nicole: No problem. Your order should be here in about ten minutes.

A. Word Definitions

Use the clues to fill in the blanks with the word choices given.

order	waitress	recommend	dish	bacon	popular	extra	add

1. Can you ____________ a movie for children? (suggest)
2. I'd like some ____________ sauce with my steak, please. (more)
3. What are you going to ____________ for dessert? (ask for)
4. My meal tastes good, but the cook should ____________ some salt next time. (put in)
5. The fried chicken is the cheapest ____________ on the menu. (food)
6. The garden salad is very ____________ with young women. (many people like it)
7. When you see the ____________, please ask her for more coffee. (restaurant worker)
8. The ____________ on that cheeseburger isn't good for you. (type of meat)

B. Meanings in Context

Choose the meaning of the sentence in the conversation.

1. I can't wait to order.
   - a. The service is so slow. Let's leave.
   - b. I'm really hungry.

2. It's our first time at this restaurant.
   - a. We haven't eaten here before.
   - b. We got here very early.

3. Hold the tomatoes, please.
   - a. I'd like some extra tomatoes.
   - b. Don't put any tomatoes on it.

4. Could you give me extra barbecue sauce on the side?
   - a. Could I have more sauce in a small dish?
   - b. Could you put less sauce on my food?

C. Language Tips

Ordering a Meal

A Waiter Might Say . . .	A Customer Might Say . . .
May I get you something to start? Are you ready to order? Our soup of the day is (kind of soup). And for your main course / drink / dessert? Do you want anything to drink? Your order should be here in a few minutes.	I'll start with / I'd like to start with (kind of starters). I would like / I'll have / I'd like to have (kind of main dishes). Does it / that come with (kind of side dishes)? What kinds of (kind of drinks) are there?

Grammar

Indefinite Pronouns

Words like **something, anybody, both,** and **any** are indefinite pronouns. We use them in place of nouns. Some indefinite pronouns can be singular or plural. When they replace a singular (plural) noun, use a singular (plural) verb.

Singular Indefinite Pronouns (use a singular verb)

something	everything	anything	nothing	someone
one	everyone/everybody	anyone/anybody	no one/nobody	another

Something smells delicious in here.
Everything is good here.
Do you want anything to drink?
Nobody knows the manager's age.
I already had a cup of coffee this morning, but I want to have another.

Plural Indefinite Pronouns (use a plural verb)

both	few	many	others	several

You should try our bacon cheeseburger and mushroom burger. Both are very popular.
A few students take the subway, but many take the bus.
The cameras are expensive. Several cost over $1,000.

Singular or Plural Indefinite Pronouns (use a singular or a plural verb)

some	any	all

Would you like to have tea? There is some in the kitchen. (singular)
The director made a lot of action movies. Some were really successful. (plural)
Could you bring a cup from the kitchen? Any is fine. (singular)
Look at those great jackets! Are any on sale? (plural)

Usage Note

Indefinite pronouns usually take the place of nouns. Some, however, can do other things in a sentence.

I have many classmates, and **some** are my best friends. (indefinite pronoun)

Some animals at the zoo are dangerous. (determiner)

Ted has two sisters, and **both** are very pretty. (indefinite pronoun)

Both apartments have a large bathroom. (determiner)

A. Fill in the Blanks

*Use the words **something, anything, nothing, somebody, anybody,** or **nobody** to complete the sentences.*

1. There's a message on the phone. Maybe ____________ wants to buy your car.
2. The machine is broken. ____________ happens when I push the button.
3. I don't know ____________ from Australia.
4. Beverly looks worried. ____________ is bothering her.
5. I went to the shopping mall, but I didn't really need ____________.
6. The bookstore was open, but ____________ was inside.

B. Match

Match the question / statement with the response.

_____	1. Not many students got good marks.	a. Yes. Another is a computer engineer.
_____	2. How many people like pizza?	b. Everything is ten percent off.
_____	3. Which one do you like?	c. Some have them.
_____	4. Several are very cheap.	d. Are any funny?
_____	5. What is on sale in the store?	e. I think everyone does.
_____	6. How many bikes in the shop have lights?	f. Both are beautiful.
_____	7. Is one of your friends a doctor?	g. Yeah. They cost less than $20.
_____	8. There are lots of movies to see.	h. That's right. Few passed the test.

C. Correct the Mistakes

Fix the errors in the article.

Cats and dogs are popular pets. Both ~~is~~ are good pets, but many people like just another. Some likes dogs and other are cat lovers. Few is fans of both.

There are many different kinds of dogs. Some weighs more than 100 pounds, while other types of dogs are small. Their hair is different too. A golden retriever's hair is long. A bulldog has short hair. Anyone loves puppies. Everything about puppies are cute. But few stays cute. They become big dogs.

Cats aren't as different as dogs. Many is the same size. However, they can be different colors. Look at the cats in a pet store. One is white. Another are black. And some is many different colors. Of course, somebody thinks kittens are cute.

Reading

Before You Read

Look at the pictures. Have you tried one of these food? Have you had any difficulties eating foods in foreign countries?

Going to Restaurants around the World

Track 51

While You Read

1. How do you pay the bill in France? How about Thailand?

2. If you don't want to have any more drinks in Japan, what should you do?

Food is an important part of a culture, and one of the best ways to enjoy it is in a local restaurant. Every culture has its own table manners. Remember that in different countries, people eat differently.

In India, most people eat with their hands. Wash your hands first! You must use the right hand to eat because Indians think that the left is not clean. Do not touch other people's food or offer them yours. Eating beef and pork is prohibited — a lot of people in India are Hindu or Muslim.

Thai food is for sharing. Don't ask for your own dish. Take enough for a bite or two and eat slowly. The oldest woman should order, and the richest person pays.

Don't pour your own drink in Japan. Your companions will pour it for you. If you don't want any more, leave your glass full. When you pay the bill in Japan, you shouldn't count your change.

French cooks don't like it when you ask for ketchup. You should try the meal first. During your meal, your hands should be visible at all times. Most French people split the bill. You should pay an equal amount, not ask everyone what they ate.

A. Words with Different Meanings

Match the word in bold with its definition.

1 Her story was reported in the **local** newspaper. ______
One of the best parts of visiting a country is talking with the **locals**. ______
Definition: ⓐ *adj.* related to a particular area ⓑ *n.* a person who lives in a particular area

2 Valerie took a big **bite** of French bread. ______
The man saw a doctor after the dog **bit** him. ______
Definition: ⓐ *v.* to cut something with your teeth ⓑ *n.* the act of using your teeth to cut something

3 We were both full after such a big dinner, so we asked for the **bill**. ______
This isn't a real 100-dollar **bill**, so the bank won't take it. ______
Definition: ⓐ *n.* paper money ⓑ *n.* a list of charges

4 Men and women should have **equal** rights. ______
The baskets have an **equal** number of Easter eggs in them. ______
Definition: ⓐ *adj.* being treated the same ⓑ *adj.* of the same size, amount, or value

B. Word Definitions

Use the clues to fill in the blanks with the word choices given. Change the word form if necessary.

offer	appropriate	pour	companion	visible	at all times	split

1. The woman might be in danger, so the police are staying outside of her house ____________. (always)
2. We should ____________ the cake into eight pieces. Everyone should get one slice. (divide)
3. It's not ____________ to wear shorts. This is a formal dinner party. (suitable)
4. Dogs are great ____________. You should get one. (friend)
5. That advertisement is ____________ from the other side of the highway. (easy to see)
6. The host ____________ Bob something to drink. (provide)
7. The waitress ____________ drinks for the customers. (fill a cup with a drink)

C. True or False

*Check **True** or **False**.*

	True	False
1. Never touch another person's dish at the table in India.	☐	☐
2. You shouldn't order a steak or some bacon in India.	☐	☐
3. The right hand is considered to be unclean in India.	☐	☐
4. In Thai culture, all dishes are shared.	☐	☐
5. In Japan, do not fill your own glass.	☐	☐
6. French chefs will be happy to offer ketchup to customers.	☐	☐
7. You shouldn't put your hands under the table in France.	☐	☐
8. French people like to share the bill.	☐	☐

UNIT 12

School Life

1. Where do you see yourself ten years from now?
2. What kind of job do you want to do?
3. Are you studying courses in school that will help you reach your goals?

Words & Expressions

Listen and write the personality words you hear in the blanks. Track 52

friendly	gentle	independent	risk taker	hardworking	generous
serious	negative	fun-loving	patient	talented	careful

Personality Traits

1.  ____________

2.  ____________

3.  ____________

4.  ____________

5.  ____________

6.  ____________

7.  ____________

8.  ____________

9.  ____________

10.  ____________

11.  ____________

12.  ____________

Practice

Talk to a partner.

- Which personality types are good?
- What do your friends say about you? Which adjectives do they use?

Listen Up

Task I *Listen and complete the sentences with the words you hear.* Track 53

Dialogue 1	**1.** John wants to change his __________ to business. **2.** Sara advises John to study __________.
Dialogue 2	**3.** Gordon needs to buy flowers for his __________. **4.** Marc __________ $100 to Gordon several days ago.
Dialogue 3	**5.** Claire plays the __________. **6.** It is sometimes difficult to find work as a(n) __________.

Task II *Listen again and write the name next to the matching personality description.*

John
Marc
Gordon
Claire

1. __________ is not confident.
2. __________ is a careful person.
3. __________ thinks Gordon is generous.
4. __________ borrowed money from Marc.
5. __________ is a hardworking person.
6. __________ likes to buy things for people.

Act It Out

Practice the conversations with the word choices given.

generous confident fun-loving risk-taking

likes to share believes in himself (herself)
loves to go to parties tries new things often

cheap negative serious careful

doesn't like to spend money is never happy
doesn't smile often seldom takes risks

1. A: Is (*name*) a __________ person?
B: Yes. He / She __________.

2. A: You are too __________ sometimes.
B: Maybe you're right.
I'm not __________ (antonym) enough.

3. A: (*Name*) is quite __________.
B: Yeah, he / she __________.

Did You Know...?

Fill in the blanks with the word choices given.

fun-loving	risk taker	talented	hardworking	make friends	risk-taking

1. He is a __________. He takes risks. He is a __________ person.
2. She is __________. She has a talent.
3. I work hard. I am a __________ person.
4. We love fun. We're a group of __________ people.
5. They are friendly. They __________ easily.

Conversation

Tell Me What to Do

Listen and fill in the blanks with the word choices given. Track 54

goal	hardworking	confident	drop	experience	trouble

A student comes into an advisor's office.

Advisor: Hi, Rachel. How can I help you?

Rachel: Hello. I'm having 1. ____________ with my schoolwork. The midterms are coming up.

Advisor: You're a 2. ____________ student. You'll do great.

Rachel: I'm taking too many classes this semester. I also have a part-time job at a bank. I aim to get some real-world 3. ____________, but I'm under a lot of stress. I'm having difficulty finding enough time to do everything.

Advisor: Can you leave your job?

Rachel: I need the money.

Advisor: If you take out student loans, you don't need to work.

Rachel: My 4. ____________ is to find a good job in finance. If I keep my job, I might make it happen.

Advisor: You should just 5. ____________ one class.

Rachel: But which class? The deadline is around the corner. I might fail all my classes!

Advisor: Don't be so negative. You should feel more 6. ____________ about yourself. Why don't you take two weeks off? If your boss likes you, he will let you.

Rachel: That's a good idea. Thanks for the advice!

A. Word Definitions

Use the clues to fill in the blanks with the word choices given. Change the word form if necessary.

midterm	semester	aim	loan	finance	deadline

1. I need to finish this paper before the final ____________. (time limit)
2. He's an expert in ____________. That's why he's rich. (economics)
3. Leslie is studying hard for her history ____________ next week. (test)
4. Rick got a big ____________ from the bank for his new car. (money you borrow)
5. I'm taking five courses this ____________. (term)
6. Matthew ____________ to finish business school in two years. (plan)

B. Meanings in Context

Choose the meaning of the sentence in the conversation.

1. The midterms are coming up.
- **a.** They are arriving in a few days.
- **b.** There are some big tests soon.

2. I'm under a lot of stress.
- **a.** I'm worried and nervous.
- **b.** I'm hungry and thirsty.

3. The deadline is around the corner.
- **a.** It's on the other side of the street.
- **b.** There isn't much time left to do it.

4. Don't be so negative.
- **a.** You should exercise more.
- **b.** You should look on the bright side.

C. Words with Different Meanings

Match the word in bold with its definition.

1 I'm having **trouble** sending e-mails from my computer. ______
Jane often **troubled** her parents to look after her baby son. ______
Definition: ⓐ *n.* difficulty ⓑ *v.* to bother

2 Water from the roof **dropped** onto my head. ______
I don't like history very much, so I **dropped** the course. ______
Definition: ⓐ *v.* to fall ⓑ *v.* to stop studying

3 Once again, my brother **failed** to arrive on time. ______
Jesse **failed** two of his exams this year. ______
Definition: ⓐ *v.* to not pass ⓑ *v.* to not do something

D. Language Tips

Discussing Problems

I'm having	trouble with + Noun / Verb + -ing. difficulty + Verb + -ing. problems + Verb + -ing. a hard time + Verb + -ing.

Noun / Verb + -ing	is / are not easy. is / are difficult. is / are giving me a headache.

Use the information to practice the sentence patterns.

(prepare for) the final exams — (finish) my history paper — (study) German
(learn) this material — (set up) the new computer software

Grammar

Conditionals

Zero Conditional

We use the **zero conditional** when we talk about thing that are always true.

If + present simple, present simple

If you heat chocolate, it melts.
= Chocolate melts if you heat it.

If you study hard, you get good grade.
= You get good grade if you study hard.

If you eat too much, you gain weight.
= You gain weight if you eat too much.

Usage Note

When or **every time** has the same meaning as **if** in some zero conditional sentences.

If / **When** / **Every time** Sally drinks milk, she gets sick.

First Conditional

We use the **first conditional** when we talk about future events for real possibilities.

If + present simple, will + verb

If I have money, I will buy a new computer.
= I will buy a new computer if I have money.

If we win a contest, we will get the prize money.
= We will get the prize money if we win a contest.

If your boss likes you, he will let you take two weeks off.
= You boss will let you take two weeks off if he likes you.

Different Forms

	Condition	Result	Usage
If	I keep my job,	I **might** / **may** make it happen.	possibility
	you use the kitchen,	you **must** / **have to** do the dishes.	obligation
	she takes a plane,	she **should** ask for a window seat.	advice
	you have a driver's license,	you **can** / **may** drive.	permission
	someone calls,	tell them to call back later.	order

A. Fill in the Blanks

Write the correct form of each verb to complete the sentences.

1. Plants __________ (die) if they __________ (not get) enough water.
2. If the weather __________ (be) nice, we __________ (go) to the park tomorrow.
3. If Emily __________ (be) late for work again, her boss __________ (get) angry.
4. If you __________ (lie) to people all the time, they __________ (not believe) you any more.
5. My teacher __________ (get) upset if the students __________ (make) noise.
6. If it __________ (rain) tomorrow, Jerry and his friends __________ (not attend) the outdoor concert.
7. If my daughter __________ (eat) spicy food, her stomach __________ (hurt).
8. Dogs __________ (bark) loudly if they __________ (see) a cat.

B. Match

Match the condition with the result.

_____ 1. If Laurie goes to bed after eleven,
_____ 2. If I get sick again,
_____ 3. If Ben doesn't have to work tomorrow,
_____ 4. If Maggie and her boyfriend sit in the front,
_____ 5. If your dad comes home before six o'clock,
_____ 6. If the room's temperature is too low,
_____ 7. If the bus is late,
_____ 8. If Bill walks to school,

a. ask him to give Uncle Bob a call.
b. I can't sleep.
c. he'll get some exercise.
d. she is tired the next day.
e. we might have to take a taxi.
f. I may need to see a doctor.
g. they will hear the music better.
h. he should come to the beach with us.

C. Correct the Mistakes

Fix the errors in the passage.

Student life can be full of stress. If students ~~won't~~ don't have a good balance between study, exercise, and rest, they usually have problems. They didn't get good grades if they relaxed too much. They don't remember as much if they not take regular breaks though.

Exercise is really important too. A student study better and feel better if they go outside and play sports. If you focusing only on study, you might get worse grades! If you wanted to do well in school, you should keep both your body and brain healthy.

Relaxed, healthy students are better learners. Remember, if you're tired, taking a break. You remember much more if you will balance your time!

Reading

Before You Read

Have you ever done an internship? Where would you like to do an internship?

Working for No Money

Track 55

While You Read

1. *Why do students work for free?*
2. *What do Vatican interns receive?*

Would you work for free? Most people would answer: "Absolutely not!" After all, it sounds unreasonable, right? However, a lot of Western college students work for no money. Instead of pay, they get experience, knowledge, and a better résumé. These jobs are called internships.

Many American university students take internships in their future fields. For example, sports or fashion majors would apply for an internship at Nike. People who are interested in film or computer science try for an internship with Pixar. There are plenty of opportunities.

Some well-known companies provide benefits with internships. Google interns have a better chance of getting a job later. Over a million people apply each year. The company usually hires just 2,000. Microsoft offers a 12-week internship. After they finish, interns can have a barbecue at Bill Gates' house! Interns for Southwest Airlines get free flights for the summer. Vatican interns report for the Catholic News Service. In return, they get free Italian lessons and the chance to live in a four-star hotel in Rome. These internships are really competitive, but they're also a great opportunity for students.

These days, internships are very popular. Ask your university about its internship program. It could change your life.

A. Word Definitions

Use the clues to fill in the blanks with the word choices given. Change the word form if necessary.

absolutely	instead of	résumé	field	apply	plenty of	well-known	competitive

1. Let's eat pizza ____________ noodles today. (as an alternative)
2. The medical ____________ is rapidly growing. (area of study)
3. My internship experience will be the most important part of my ____________. (a list of achievements)
4. Dan's father is a(n) ____________ Canadian actor. (famous)
5. You should ____________ for a visa two months before you travel. (request)
6. I ____________ love my job. The pay is good, and my boss is great. (certainly)
7. Professional football is a very ____________ sport. (have a strong desire to win)
8. There are ____________ people in the park. (many)

B. Complete the Passage

Use the correct form of the words given to complete the passage.

experience	major	intern	benefit	internship

College is the best time in most people's lives. From drama to computer science 1. ____________, college students can study all kinds of things. They study hard during the semester. Then students have vacation between each semester. Some students spend their summers traveling or relaxing, but today many of them want to do a(n) 2. ____________ in big companies. The job market isn't great, and a little real-world 3. ____________ can be an advantage. 4. ____________ can see how a company works. They gain a good understanding of what the job is. Another 5. ____________ is that they have a better chance of finding work when they finish college. Many companies prefer new employees with previous work experience.

C. True or False

*Check **True** or **False**.*

	True	False
1. Interns usually get paid a lot for their work.	☐	☐
2. Nike is a good choice for a fashion internship.	☐	☐
3. Film majors can go for an internship at Pixar.	☐	☐
4. There are not many types of internships available.	☐	☐
5. Google hires more than 3,000 workers per year.	☐	☐
6. Vatican interns get free flights once they finish their internships.	☐	☐
7. Universities usually have information on internships.	☐	☐
8. Students can get a lot of benefits from doing internships.	☐	☐

Writing

STUDENT BOOK 2

Writing

Task I *Below is a profile of Jenny and a short paragraph about her. Fill in the blanks.*

Name: Jenny Collins
Sex: female
Age: 18
School: New York University
Major: nursing
Year at school: freshman
Languages: English, French

Clubs: guitar, drama
Hobbies: playing the guitar, acting, singing, playing tennis
Favorite movie: *Alice in Wonderland*
Favorite TV show: *Glee*
Favorite singer / band: Radiohead
Favorite song: *Karma Police*
Future plans: work at a hospital

My name is ________________. I'm ________________ (age). I'm a student in my ________ year at ________________. I study ________________. I love my school! I have a lot of hobbies. I'm a member of the ________________________. I like to ________________, ________________, ____________, and ________________ in my free time. I enjoy watching movies. I like ________________ the most. I also watch TV shows sometimes. My favorite program is __________. Music is very important to me. I usually listen to rock music. ___________ is the best band in the world! I really love their song ______________. After I graduate, I want to ________________.

Task II *Fill in this profile. Write a short paragraph about yourself. Use Jenny's paragraph as an example.*

Put Photo Here

Name: ________________
Sex: __________ Age: _____
School: ________________________________
Major: ______________ Year at school: ______________
Language(s): ________________________________

____

____

____

____

____

Writing

Task I *Read this introduction to Thanksgiving.*

Thanksgiving is an important holiday in the United States and Canada. People celebrate the Pilgrims' successful journey from Europe to the New World in 1621. Thanksgiving takes place in November. People meet with their entire family, cook a lot of food, and eat together. Many people live far away from each other, but they still try to get together on Thanksgiving Day. Traditional Thanksgiving foods include turkey, potatoes, sweet potatoes, sweet corn, and pumpkin pie. It's a day to eat a lot and relax with your family.

Use the introduction above as a sample. Write a short passage about Dragon Boat Festival. Make sure to answer the following questions.

1. What is Dragon Boat Festival?
2. When do people celebrate this festival?
3. What do people usually do (for example, race dragon boats, prepare rice dumplings, etc.)?
4. What are some of the traditional foods? What are they made of?

____

____

____

____

____

Task II *Look at the recipe below. Fill in the blanks using the words in the box.*

Thanksgiving Recipe: Sweet Potatoes

sweet potatoes	mix	make	bake	heat	place	add

To **1.** __________ this dish, you need a bowl of **2.** __________, a quarter of a cup of orange juice, three quarters of a cup of flour, half a cup of sugar, some butter, and half a spoon of salt. **3.** __________ the oven to 175 degrees. Put the sweet potatoes in a dish. **4.** __________ them in the oven. **5.** __________ some orange juice. **6.** __________ sugar, butter, flour, and salt together in a bowl. Pour everything from the bowl on the sweet potatoes. **7.** __________ for 30 to 40 minutes.

Create a recipe of your own and share it with the class.

Writing

Internet Language

Many people use Internet language when they talk online.

2: to
2day: today
2morrow: tomorrow
2nite: tonight
aite: alright
asap: as soon as possible
c: see
cmon: come on
cya: see you
h8: hate
h/w: homework
iasb: I am so bored
idk: I don't know
k: OK
kewl: cool
l8r: later
lol: laugh out loud
nm: not much
ntrly: not really
sup: what's up
syatp: see you at the party
pleez: please
thx: thanks
tmw: too much work
ur: you're
urtb: you are the best
wanna: want to

Change the conversation below into regular language.

Adam: Hey, Eva. Sup?
Eva: Nm. U?
Adam: I'm tired. I have h/w 2 do for 2morrow. ☹
Eva: Is it a lot?
Adam: Ntrly, but I just h8 math.
Eva: Ur so lazy! Lol. 😜 Wanna go c a movie 2nite?
Adam: Idk. I have tmw right now.
Eva: Pleez? Iasb 2day.
Adam: Aite. Let me finish my h/w first. Can I call u l8r?
Eva: Kewl. Let me know asap.

Change the following conversation into Internet language.

Kate: I am having a party tonight. You're invited. Bring your friends too!
Sam: Sounds cool. But I have classes tomorrow morning.
Kate: Come on. I need you there. You can come for a few hours.
Sam: OK, I will.
Kate: Thanks! You are the best. 😁
Sam: Alright. See you at the party.
Kate: OK. See you later then.

Writing

Task I *An ad company is looking for new models. Fill in the blanks using words from this unit.*

A

Model Needed

We are looking for a female model for a beer advertisement. She should be **1. s**__________ (she can't be overweight). We need someone **2. y**__________ (between 18 and 24 years old). She should have **3. l**__________, **4. s**__________, **5. b**__________ hair. She can't have short, curly, or black hair.

B

Man Wanted for Ad

A car company needs a male model for a sales video. We want someone **1. t**__________. His height should be at least 180 centimeters. He can have **2. l**__________ or **3. s**__________ hair. The length of his hair is not important. We also need someone **4. f**__________. He should have a big, strong body.

C

Lost Your Hair? Work for Us!

HAIR4U is looking for an actor for a hair product ad. He must be at least 50 years old. He also should be **1. b**__________. He can't have much hair. He can be **2. t**__________ or **3. s**__________. His height doesn't matter. It's OK for him to be a little **4. o**__________, but he shouldn't be too fat.

Task II *Choose one product from below. Pretend you need a model for an ad. Write an ad like the ones above.*

Title: ____________________

____

____

____

____

____

Writing

Task I *You are a nurse. Fill in the blanks in the note.*

health problem	symptoms	treatment
back injury	back pain hard to move hurts to stand	bed rest for a week cold pack twice a day massage slow exercises aspirin, two pills, three times a day with food

Note:

The patient has a back injury. He has a lot of **1.** __________. He also finds it difficult **2.** __________. His back **3.** __________ when he stands. He needs to **4.** __________ in bed for **5.** __________ days. He should also take two **6.** __________ of aspirin with **7.** __________, **8.** __________ each day. He might want to get a(n) **9.** __________ and do **10.** __________.

Task II *Answer the following questions and write a complete paragraph. Use some of the expressions below.*

once a year every (*number*) years / months / weeks	yesterday last month / year / winter two months ago in July / 2018	runny nose fever cough sore throat muscle pain	don't go to work / school rest in bed have a lot of water drink orange juice eat soup get more sleep avoid public places

a. How often do you get a cold?

b. When was the last time you had a cold?

c. What symptoms did you have?

d. What did the doctor tell you to do?

e. What did you do to feel better when you were sick?

f. What medicine did you take? How often did you take it? How much did you take?

g. How long did it take you to get healthy?

Read your paragraph to a partner. Help each other to fix any mistakes.

Writing

Task I

Below are reviews of two movies. Use the words from the box to fill in the blanks.

funny	movie theater	runs	about	leading actors
should	boring	directed	comedy	action

A *Little Fockers* Review

This movie is the third in a series. The **1.** ________________ in this movie are Ben Stiller and Robert De Niro. Paul Weitz is the director. This movie is **2.** ________________ a married couple with two children. The father of the children works with a beautiful woman. That woman is interested in him. This is a(n) **3.** ________________. The actors are pretty good, but some of the jokes are not **4.** ________________. It's not a bad movie, but you shouldn't go to the **5.** ________________ to watch it. You can watch it at home.

B *Harry Potter and the Deathly Hallows* Review

This is the seventh Harry Potter movie. It stars Daniel Radcliffe and Emma Watson. It is a story about a school of wizards. Harry Potter prepares to fight his enemy Lord Voldemort. The film was **1.** ________________ by David Yates. He did a good job. It **2.** ________________ for two and a half hours. That's a bit too long. That's why parts of the movie are a little **3.** ________________. Other parts are still a lot of fun. There are many fights and great **4.** ________________ scenes. If you like Harry Potter, you **5.** ________________ see this movie.

Task II

Choose a movie and write a review. Answer the questions in complete sentences.

a. What is the movie about?

b. Who are the stars of the movie?

c. Who is the director of the movie?

d. What kind of movie is it (action, comedy, drama, etc.)?

e. What do you think about the movie? Is it boring, exciting, or intelligent?

f. Should people spend money and go to see it? Why or why not?

________________________ *(Movie Name)* **Review**

____

____

____

____

____

____

____

Writing

Task I

Read these descriptions of special moments in Rick's life. Fill in the blanks using the words below.

interesting	lonely	friend	nervous	thankful
cheer	worried	happiest	proud	saddest

A

The **1.** ____________ day of my life was when my dog Leo died. That was four years ago. He was very sick. I was really **2.** ____________ about him.

One week later, he passed away. He was more than just a dog. He was my best **3.** ____________. I felt **4.** ____________ without him. I cried a lot. My friends helped to **5.** ____________ me up. They called me every day. I felt **6.** ____________ to them. It's good to have friends when you feel sad.

B

My first day at the university was the **1.** ____________ day of my life. My parents were very **2.** ____________ of me. They always expected me to be successful. I met my roommates at the dorms. They were both **3.** ____________ people. It felt fantastic to make new friends. I was excited to start school. I was also **4.** ____________. This was my first time away from home. I finally became an adult.

Task II

Complete Rick's story of his scary experience. Use the hints and your imagination.

The scariest time of my life was when I got lost in a forest. It happened when I was 19. I went hiking alone. I didn't pay attention to the time. *(Now finish the story.)*

a. ____ (dark)

b. ____ (scared)

c. ____ (cold)

d. ____ (freezing to death)

e. ____ (warm cave)

f. ____ (fell asleep)

g. ____ (morning, find, road)

h. ____ (car)

i. ____ (gave, ride home)

j. ____ (happy, relieved)

Task I *Write about your free-time activity. Use the sentence patterns below.*

1. What is the activity?	In my free time, I enjoy + Verb + -ing. My favorite activity is + Verb + -ing.
2. Whom do you do it with?	I usually + Verb with my friends. My family and I often + Verb on the weekend.
3. Why do you like it?	I like + Noun / Verb + -ing + because . . . Noun / Verb + -ing is fun.
4. How often do you do it?	I + Verb + three times a week. I spend every weekend + Verb + -ing.
5. How much does it cost?	I spend (*money*) every time I + Verb. It costs (*money*) to Verb.

____

____

____

____

____

Task II *Janet is writing an e-mail to Mike. Fill in the blanks.*

discount	hip-hop	club	plan	free	pop	once	clubbing	charge

Hey Mike,

How are you? Are you **1.** __________ this weekend? I know you like to party. I often go **2.** __________ with my friends on Saturdays because I like to dance. Would you like to come to a **3.** __________ with us this weekend? There is a cool place near my house. They play **4.** __________ music and **5.** __________. I go there at least **6.** __________ a month. The cover **7.** __________ is $20, but I know the owner. We would get a **8.** __________. We spend around $10 every time we go. Dancing is always fun. Does this sound like a **9.** __________? Let me know ASAP.

Best regards,

Janet

Writing

Task I *Look at Cristiano Ronaldo's profile. Fill in the blanks with the information given.*

Cristiano Ronaldo

Photo: nimAdestiny / Flickr

Sport	Soccer
Nationality	Portuguese
Position	Forward, midfielder
Former club Years	Manchester United 2003 — 2009
Current club Years	Real Madrid 2009 — present
Awards	FIFA's Player of the Year, 2008 Three Premier League championships One Champions League cup
Annual salary	About $18,000,000

Biography

Cristiano Ronaldo is a famous **1.** __________ soccer player. He plays for **2.** __________. He also played for Manchester United from **3.** __________ to **4.** __________. He **5.** __________ three Premier League championships and a Champions League cup. He received FIFA's Player of the Year Award in 2008. Ronaldo makes about $18 **6.** __________ a year.

Task II *Work with a partner to complete the following conversation. Use the words given.*

Sport
soccer
basketball
baseball

Position
goalkeeper, forward, midfielder, defender
guard, forward, center
pitcher, catcher, first base, second base, third base

A: What is your favorite sport?

B: ______________________. What's yours?

A: I really like ______________________.

B: That's cool. Do you play or watch?

A: I ______________________.

B: Which ______________________ (team, favorite)?

A: ______________________. What about you?

B: ______________________.

Who ______________________ (favorite, player)?

A: I'm a huge fan of ______________________.

He ______________________ (position). And you?

B: My favorite ______________________.

He ______________________ (position).

Writing

Task I *Use the correct form of the words to fill in the blanks in the report about a snowstorm.*

snow	temperature	die	avoid	damage
prepare	experience	wind	last	cover

Our town **1.** __________ a snowstorm last week. The **2.** __________ was minus 15 degrees Celsius. We had heavy **3.** __________ and strong **4.** __________. It was blowing at a speed of 120 kilometers per hour, so we couldn't see anything. The roads were **5.** __________ by snow. Driving was impossible. There was some **6.** __________ to the power lines, and many people didn't have electricity. Lots of trees fell down. Luckily, we were warned about the storm and were **7.** __________. We bought food and water ahead of time. Everybody **8.** __________ going outside. The storm **9.** __________ for two days. Many houses were damaged by the wind and the snow. The good news is that nobody **10.** __________!

Task II *Imagine that your city will be hit by a typhoon. Write a weather warning in **the future tense**.*

This is a weather warning. ____________________ (reach, tomorrow)

____________________ (rain, thunder, lightning)

____________________ (200 millimeters of rain)

____________________ (wind, strong, speed, 140 kilometers)

____________________ (dangerous)

____________________ (need, food, water)

____________________ (probably, no electricity)

____________________ (buy, flashlight)

____________________ (radio, weather reports)

____________________ (updates, 30 minutes)

Stay safe out there.

Writing

Task I *Below is a restaurant review. Use the correct form of the words to fill in the blanks.*

date	dessert	starter	service	parking	favorite
baked	recommend	open	salty	accept	wine

La Parisienne is a new French restaurant. I went there last week. The waiter **1.** ___________ the onion soup and the duck breast with **2.** ___________ potatoes. I accepted his suggestion. I also ordered a tomato salad as a(n) **3.** ___________. It was great. The onion soup was tasty but a little **4.** ___________. The duck was perfectly cooked. That was my **5.** ___________ dish of the night. For **6.** ___________, I had a piece of chocolate cake. I loved it. I washed my meal down with a nice glass of **7.** ___________. It was an excellent dining experience. This is not a cheap restaurant, but it's a good place for a(n) **8.** ___________.

General Info:

The **9.** ___________ is friendly and quick. The restaurant **10.** ___________ all credit cards. It takes reservations over the phone or online. There is **11.** ___________ in the back. It's **12.** ___________ from Monday to Saturday, from noon to 10:00 p.m.

Task II *Write a review of your favorite restaurant. Answer the following questions in your review.*

1. What type of food does it serve?
2. What is the most popular dish there?
3. What is your favorite (least favorite) dish, and why do (don't) you like it?
4. What is the best starter? How about dessert?
5. What general info can you provide?

____

____

____

____

____

____

____

____

____

____

____

Writing

Task I *Below is an ad for an internship. Use the correct form of the words to fill in the blanks.*

hardworking	intern	succeed	experience
résumé	interest	attitude	call

INTERNS NEEDED

BrandMark Inc. is a popular marketing company. With more than 30 years of **1.** __________, we provide **2.** __________ with lots of training. If you work for us, you will develop important real-world skills.

The perfect intern must have a(n) **3.** __________ in business development. He or she shouldn't be lazy — we want someone **4.** __________. Applicants need to have a positive **5.** __________ and try hard to **6.** __________. They must major in Business. If this is you, send a(n) **7.** __________ and a cover letter to David Gunning at dgunning@brandmark.com. No phone **8.** __________, please.

Task II *Fill in the cover letter using the information in the ad above.*

Ken Carter
Résumé

Goal:
To find an internship in marketing

Education:
Brown University
B.A. in Business expected June 2017

Work Experience:
March 2014 to September 2014
Store Manager, Iscream, Providence

- Managed three salespeople
- Created business reports
- Helped to increase sales

School Record:
Third out of 120 in the Department of Business

Dear ______________,

I am ______________________________ (student). I will ______________ (2017). I saw your ad online. I am interested in becoming an intern at your company. ______________________________ (top three). I study hard to get good grades, and I have a strong interest in business. I also ______________ ______________ (attitude). If I see a problem, I do everything to solve it. In addition, I have business experience. From March to September 2014, I worked as ______________ ______________ (Iscream). During my time there, I ______________, ______________, and ______________. I would be a great intern at BrandMark Inc. I hope to hear from you soon.

Best regards,

____

NOTES

NOTES

NOTES